Twayne's Filmmakers Series

Warren French
EDITOR

Joseph L. Mankiewicz

Joseph L. Mankiewicz

BERNARD F. DICK
Fairleigh Dickinson University

BOSTON

Twayne Publishers

1983

Joseph L. Mankiewicz

is first published in 1983 by Twayne Publishers,
A Division of G. K. Hall & Company
All Rights Reserved

Copyright © 1983 by G. K. Hall & Company

Book Production by John Amburg

Printed on permanent/durable acid-free paper and bound
in the United States of America

First Printing, October 1983

Library of Congress Cataloging in Publication Data

Dick, Bernard F.
Joseph L. Mankiewicz.

(Twayne's filmmakers series)
Bibliography: p. 167
Filmography: p. 169
Includes index.
1. Mankiewicz, Joseph L.   I. Title.   II. Series.
PN1998.A3M31975   1983   791.43'0233'0924 83-8434
ISBN 0-8057-9291-0

Contents

About the Author

BERNARD F. DICK was born in Scranton, Pennsylvania, on 25 November 1935. He holds a B.A. in Classics from the University of Scranton and a Ph.D. in classics from Fordham University. He has taught at Iona College where he chaired the Classics Department from 1967 to 1970. Since 1970, he has been at Fairleigh Dickinson University (Teaneck-Hackensack Campus) where he is professor of English and comparative literature, teaching courses in film history and criticism, literary theory, and world literature.

His books include *William Golding* (1967), *The Hellenism of Mary Renault* (1972), *The Apostate Angel: A Critical Study of Gore Vidal* (1974), *Anatomy of Film* (1978), *Billy Wilder* (1980), and *Hellman in Hollywood* (1982). He has also edited the screenplay of *Dark Victory* (1981) for the Wisconsin/Warner Brothers Screenplay Series.

His monograph on Lillian Hellman appears in supplement 1 of *Scribner's American Writers* (1978). His essays, articles, and reviews have appeared in the *Saturday Review, Georgia Review, Colorado Quarterly, Literature/Film Quarterly, Quarterly Review of Film Studies, Comparative Literature*, and *World Literature Today*. He has presented papers at meetings of the Modern Language Association, the Society for Cinema Studies, the American Comparative Literature Association, and the Popular Culture Association.

He is married to Katherine M. Restaino, dean of St. Peter's College at Englewood Cliffs, New Jersey.

Editor's Foreword

JOSEPH L. MANKIEWICZ has often been so exclusively associated with his classic *All about Eve* (1950) that stylistic and thematic consistencies in the twenty feature films that he directed between 1946 and 1972 have often been overlooked. Bernard Dick's book seeks to rectify this unbalanced situation and to indicate the ways in which Mankiewiez, although trained in the American studio system, was responsible for a quarter century's work that entitles him to careful consideration as an *auteur,* though rarely an entirely successful one. Indeed, one of the advantages of auteurist criticism is that it provides a vehicle for speculating on reasons why an intense and dedicated artist like Mankiewicz failed to equal the achievement of a John Ford or Howard Hawks.

As Bernard Dick points out discerningly in his examination of several of the films, Mankiewicz displayed a tendency toward excess that was often curbed by a producer like Darryl F. Zanuck, making Mankiewicz's eight years with Twentieth Century-Fox the peak of his career. When he was able to function as his own producer *and* screenwriter as in *The Barefoot Contessa* (1954) and *The Quiet American* (1958), Mankiewicz tended to overelaborate, as Dick demonstrates especially in his account of the flashbacks in the first-named film. Mankiewicz was not his own best critic; yet he occupied a singular position in Hollywood—as Dick further explains—because of his persistent interest in humanistic themes about man's self-dramatization and his "civilized" approach to subject matter that others might have sensationalized.

Mankiewicz began his directorial career rather late, after World War II, when he was thirty-seven years old and had already enjoyed successful careers as a producer at MGM under Irving Thalberg and as a scriptwriter. (Indeed, Dick devotes special attention to *The Keys of the Kingdom*—Mankiewicz's first film for Zanuck and the only one at Fox before he turned director—as a specially significant key to his techniques.) He began the work for which he is principally remembered as an already experienced artist ready to exploit subtly the gradually diminishing control of external censors over what could be exhibited on the screen. His career as a director serves, therefore, as a particularly useful guide to the problems facing Hollywood filmmakers as a new age—dominated by the threat from television to film's very survival—transformed their art.

Although Bernard Dick begins with a chronological examination of Mankiewicz's films, he early abandons this rigid plan, flashing back and forth over a quarter century (a technique peculiarly appropriate to his subject) in order to discuss the relationships of nine groups (mostly pairs, since Mankiewicz rarely committed himself for long to any single pattern) to the themes and genres that most intrigued the director. The plan culminates, as a study of Mankiewicz should, by pairing his most important work, *All about Eve*, with his apparent swan song, *Sleuth* (1972), as supreme exemplars of his preponderating tendency to explore life as theater.

Along the way, he perhaps most arrests our attention with his detailed and sympathetic discussion of the ill-starred *Cleopatra* (1963). So many words have been wasted on the length and excessive cost of the film and on the scandalous behavior of its co-stars that it has rarely been contemplated as an example of the culmination of techniques that the director developed elsewhere. Bernard Dick sees the film as ultimately poetic cinema that raises the ageless romance to the level of poetic drama without actually employing dialogue in verse.

Generally eschewing dogmatic judgments, Dick seeks to make readers aware of the strengths and weaknesses of Mankiewicz's powerfully theatrical sensibility as he struggled to reconcile literate theater with the visual requirements of *moving* pictures. Whatever place Mankiewicz finally occupies in the hierarchy of filmmakers, Dick points out that it should be based on more than the celebrity of *All about Eve* (accentuated as it has been by comparatively infrequent revivals of most of Mankiewicz's other characteristic works) and provides us with new insights that need to be considered in arriving at any judgment.

W. F.

Preface

THERE IS A SCENE in *The Quiet American*, Mankiewicz's controversial film version of Graham Greene's novel, in which the American is trying to propose to Phuong, the mistress of the British journalist Fowler, who is acting as translator. Fowler occupies a wicker chair, back of frame; Phuong sits on the floor behind the American, who stands in the center. When Phuong asks for explanations of words like "dishonor" and "future," Mankiewicz cuts to her peering from behind the American's legs; suggesting that she may be in an even more subservient position with the American than she was with Fowler.

If the same scene had occurred in someone else's film, it would have been lauded as visual irony. But one does not associate the visual with Joseph L. Mankiewicz; he is the playwright of the movies, the creator of Margo Channing, the epigrammatist responsible for "Fasten your seatbelts. It's going to be a bumpy night." Intelligence, wit, and aphoristic dialogue are Mankiewicz's legacy to film.

However, while one may remember lines like "if you've known one Albanian, you've known them all" (James Mason to Danielle Darrieux in *Five Fingers*), one also remembers pure images such as Ava Gardner dancing with the proud abandon of unobserved royalty in *The Barefoot Contessa*; the myriad reflections of Barbara Bates as she bows before a three-mirrored cheval at the end of *All about Eve*; Gene Tierney and Rex Harrison walking out a door that closes behind them as they enter a new life in *The Ghost and Mrs. Muir*. Mankiewicz is clearly a painter of pictures as well as a wielder of words. Yet one would never know it from his interviews in which he emphasized the script almost to the exclusion of everything else; describing his films as intended for "an audience as capable of listening to a film as it is of seeing it"; enjoying the reputation of being a maker of films that radiate the aura and brilliance of the theater; and boasting that his movies would have succeeded on the stage if he had written them as plays. The truth of the matter—as this study hopes to demonstrate—is that Mankiewicz's films could never have succeeded in any other medium than the one for which they were created; and that Mankiewicz himself could never have achieved the same degree of excellence in the theater as he did in the movies.

It is impossible to write about Joseph L. Mankiewicz without discussing the role that Darryl F. Zanuck played in his career. For the eight years (1943–51) that Mankiewicz was at Twentieth Century-Fox, Zanuck was vice-president in charge of production. While Mankiewicz could have been a distinguished filmmaker at any studio, it was not coincidental that the period of his best work coincided with his tenure at Fox. Zanuck's memos, which I read at Fox during the summer of 1980, reveal him as the kind of producer who scrutinized each screenplay, offering suggestions and asking for changes that, when made, usually improved the quality of the film. He repeatedly curbed Mankiewicz's tendency toward excess by requesting deletions of characters, scenes, and lines. In the case of *The Ghost and Mrs. Muir,* Zanuck was definitely off base; but, for the most part, following Zanuck's instructions—and Mankiewicz generally did—could mean the difference between a good film and an outstanding one. Mankiewicz made both.

This book is dedicated to Martin Nocente.

BERNARD F. DICK

Fairleigh Dickinson University

Acknowledgments

I WOULD LIKE to express my gratitude to Mrs. Mary McMahon, periodicals librarian at Fairleigh Dickinson University (Teaneck-Hackensack Campus) for procuring articles for me that were not readily available; Joseph and Rosemary Mankiewicz for a memorable afternoon at their Bedford, New York, home; my wife Katherine M. Restaino, but for whom research would be a rather lonely business; Margaret Riddle of the Visual Materials Library of the United Nations for arranging a viewing of *Carol for Another Christmas;* the staff of the Margaret Herrick Library of the Academy of Motion Picture Arts and Sciences in Los Angeles who make a researcher feel like a member of a family; Emily Sieger of the Motion Picture Section of the Library of Congress who, as always, provided ideal facilities for viewing the films; Sister Jeanne Tierney, C.S.J.P. of St. Peter's College at Englewood Cliffs for obtaining copies of the novels and stories that Mankiewicz adapted for the screen; Claire Townsend, former vice-president (production) at Twentieth Century-Fox, for allowing me to visit the studio in the summer of 1980 in order to read Mankiewicz's shooting scripts and Darryl F. Zanuck's memos; and Jack Yaeger, former head of story files at Fox, for finding me a place on soundstage 7 to read this material in the most natural setting imaginable. My thanks to them all; this book could not have been written without them.

Chronology

1909   Joseph Leo Mankiewicz born on 11 February in Wilkes-Barre, Pennsylvania, third child of Franz and Johanna Mankiewicz.

1913   Mankiewiczes move to New York.

1920   Graduates from P.S. 64 in New York.

1924   Graduates from Stuyvesant High School; enters Columbia University.

1928   Graduates from Columbia with major in English. Takes job at UFA in Berlin, translating German intertitles.

1929   Hired as titler by Paramount. Writes titles for silent versions of *The Dummy, Close Harmony, The Man I Love, The Studio Murder Mystery, Thunderbolt, River of Romance, The Mysterious Dr. Fu Manchu, The Saturday Night Kid, The Virginian.* Writes dialogue for *Fast Company.*

1930   *Slightly Scarlet* (co-screenplay and dialogue), *The Social Lion* (adaptation and dialogue).

1931   *Only Saps Work* (dialogue), *The Gang Buster* (dialogue), *Finn and Hattie* (dialogue); co-dialogue credit for *June Moon, Skippy, Newly Rich (Forbidden Adventure), Sooky.* Oscar nomination for *Skippy.*

1932   *This Reckless Age* (scenario and dialogue), *Sky Bride* (scenario and dialogue), *Million Dollar Legs* (co-screenplay and story); *If I Had a Million* (screenplay for "Rollo and the Roadhogs," co-screenplay of "The Three Marines"; stories for "The China Shop," "The Streetwalker," and "The Forger").

1933   *Diplomaniacs* (co-screenplay and story), *Emergency Call* (co-screenplay), *Too Much Harmony* (screenplay), *Alice in Wonderland* (co-screenplay). Hired as writer by MGM.

1934 *Manhattan Melodrama* (co-screenplay), *Our Daily Bread* (dialogue), *Forsaking All Others* (screenplay). Marries Elizabeth Young.

1935 *I Live My Life* (screenplay). Begins producing at MGM.

1936 Produces *Three Godfathers, Fury, The Gorgeous Hussy, Love on the Run.* Son Eric born.

1937 Produces *The Bride Wore Red, Double Wedding, Mannequin.* Divorces Elizabeth Young Mankiewicz.

1938 Produces *Three Comrades,* revising Fitzgerald's script; *The Shopworn Angel, The Shining Hour, A Christmas Carol.*

1939 Produces *The Adventures of Huckleberry Finn.* Marries Rosa Stradner.

1940 Produces *Strange Cargo* and *The Philadelphia Story.* Son Christopher born.

1941 Produces *The Wild Man of Borneo* and *The Feminine Touch.* Father Franz dies.

1942 Produces *Woman of the Year, Cairo* (uncredited), *Reunion in France.* Son Thomas born.

1943 Begins eight-year association with Twentieth Century-Fox.

1944 *The Keys of the Kingdom* (producer and co-screenplay).

1946 Directs first film, *Dragonwyck* (also screenplay); *Somewhere in the Night* (director, co-screenplay).

1947 Directs *The Late George Apley* and *The Ghost and Mrs. Muir.*

1948 Directs *Escape.*

1949 *A Letter to Three Wives* (director and screenplay); *House of Strangers* (director).

1950 *No Way Out* (director and co-screenplay); *All about Eve* (director and screenplay). Academy Awards for *A Letter to Three Wives* in categories of direction and writing. Elected to presidency of Screen Directors Guild. Triumphs over De Mille's attempt to recall him as SDG president.

1951 *People Will Talk* (director and screenplay). Academy Awards for *All about Eve* in categories of direction, writing, sound recording, and costume design (black and white). Leaves Fox.

1952 Directs *La Bohème* at Metropolitan Opera.

1953   *Julius Caesar* (director). Death of brother Herman.

1954   *The Barefoot Contessa* (director, producer, screenplay). Academy Award for *Julius Caesar* in category of art direction–set decoration (black and white)

1955   *Guys and Dolls* (director and screenplay). Edmond O'Brien wins Oscar for Best Supporting Actor (*The Barefoot Contessa*).

1958   *The Quiet American* (director, producer, screenplay). Suicide of Rosa Stradner Mankiewicz.

1959   *Suddenly, Last Summer* (director).

1960   Retrospective at British Film Institute in London.

1962   Marries Rosemary Matthews.

1963   *Cleopatra* (director, co-screenplay).

1964   Directs and produces *Carol for Another Christmas* for television.

1966   Birth of daughter Alexandra Kate.

1967   *The Honey Pot* (director, screenplay, co-producer). Two-week retrospective at Cinémathèque Française.

1969   *There Was a Crooked Man* (director and producer).

1972   *Sleuth* (director). Academy Award nominations for best actor (Caine and Olivier) and best director.

1974   Retrospective at fourth U.S.A. Film Festival at Southern Methodist University.

1975   Retrospective at nineteenth annual San Francisco International Film Festival.

1981   Tribute to Mankiewicz by Directors Guild of America at Museum of Modern Art in New York.

1982   Joins Elia Kazan and Arthur Penn to form Playwright/Directors Unit at Actors Studio.

1983   American member of International Jury at Berlin Film Festival.

1

From the Yellow Wood
To the Yellow Brick Road

A Life for the Movies

THEY COULD HAVE been a family in a screenplay. The father, Franz Mankiewicz, emigrated from Germany in 1892, living first in New York and then moving to Wilkes-Barre, Pennsylvania, in 1904 to take a job editing a German-language newspaper. But Franz aspired to something higher—to a college professorship which, at the turn of the century, seemed an unattainable goal for a man in his thirties without any teaching experience. However, destiny intervened in 1906 in the form of an opening for a language instructor at Wilkes-Barre's Harry Hillman Academy. Then it was on to New York for the Mankiewiczes where a position awaited Franz at Stuyvesant High School. He quickly earned an M.A. from Columbia in 1915 and a Ph.D. in education from New York University in 1924. Finally, in 1931, at the age of fifty-nine, Franz realized his life's ambition: he became a professor at City College.

The career of Herman Jacob Mankiewicz, the oldest child of Franz and Johanna, is also the stuff of which scenarios are made—tragic scenarios, not morally edifying ones. Herman suffered the fate of the firstborn from whom perfection is always expected; from whom a grade of 92 is unacceptable when 100 is the norm. Herman literally lived in the shadow of his father who taught him at the Harry Hillman Academy and enrolled at Columbia University to pursue graduate study at the same time Herman matriculated for his B.A.

Herman was expected to continue the Mankiewicz saga of intellectual attainment. He began as a writer, a prolific and respected one, who was equally adept at political reporting and theater criticism and whose wit insured him a place at the Algonquin Round Table. Herman hoped to be a playwright, collaborating with George S. Kaufman on *The Good Fellow* (1926) and with Marc Connelly on *The Wild Man of Borneo*

(1927), both of which were failures. Thus, when Hollywood beckoned with an offer to write for Paramount Pictures, he left for the West Coast, becoming head of Paramount's scenario department in 1927. At least he would be working in a quasi-literary capacity, progressing from stories and titles for silent films to screenplays with the coming of sound. Although Herman J. Mankiewicz wrote the script of what many consider the quintessentially American film, *Citizen Kane* (1941), like the traveler in Frost's "The Road Not Taken," he always lamented the choice he made in the yellow wood. Herman "lived with the knowledge that his intellectual life was irrelevant";[1] he died in 1953, convinced that he had wasted his talent in Hollywood.

The movies also played a role in the life of Erna Mankiewicz, who was born four years after Herman. Of the three Mankiewicz children, Erna alone emulated her father by entering the teaching profession; earning a B.A. from Hunter and an M.A. from Columbia, she entered the New York City system, teaching for many years at James Monroe High School. Herman, who was expected to recruit talented screenwriters for Paramount, arranged for the studio to hire his sister in 1929. However, writing for the movies was not Erna's forte; Paramount fired her after two years, and she returned to the classroom. Yet when she retired from teaching, she did publicity for United Artists and other film companies in Europe.

The youngest Mankiewicz, Joseph Leo, was born in 1909, twelve years after Herman. He would also enter the movie industry. Although Herman's reputation facilitated his entrée into films, Joseph soon acquired a name of his own. In the wax-and-wane tradition of *A Star Is Born*, as Herman descended from the summit of *Citizen Kane* to the foothills of *A Woman's Secret* (1949) and *The Pride of St. Louis* (1952), Joseph rose from an obscure titler of silent movies to one of the most celebrated screenwriter-directors in American film.

Since Franz moved his family to New York in 1913, Joseph never knew the small-town boyhood that his brother did. That Joseph grew up in New York explains something of his preference for the East where he has lived since 1951. Perhaps his choice was influenced by the equation: East Coast = cultural activity / West Coast = cultural sterility. At any rate, like his brother, he contemplated a life in letters, envisioning a career that combined university teaching with playwriting. After graduating from Columbia in 1928, Joseph was expected to make the grand tour, read English at Oxford, and return to his alma mater as a specialist in the literature of the English Renaissance. But the grand tour ended in Berlin where Joseph was dazzled by a decadence that appealed as much to the mind as it did to the senses. He would not be returning to Morningside Heights. Through one of his brother's contacts, he found a job at UFA providing English translations for intertitles in German films intended for British and American release, thus beginning in the industry as his brother did—as a titler.

On the basis of his UFA experience, Joseph was working in Hollywood within a year, writing the titles for Paramount films that were made as talkies but would be shown in theaters that were not yet equipped for sound. Joseph always claimed that he entered the movies along with sound. For with sound came the spoken word; and with the spoken word, dialogue. Neither Herman nor Joseph could have flourished in the silent era, although titling had become something of an art under Douglas Fairbanks, who gave titles wit and style, and D. W. Griffith, who used them for a variety of purposes: definitions, explanations, actual utterances, secret thoughts, and transitional links. Still, titles were no substitute for creative dialogue.

As Joseph moved from titling to dialogue and finally to screenwriting, it seemed as if he were following Herman's example, although he was really pursuing the only course a writer could in the early days of sound. Between 1929 and 1932, Joseph contributed to the scripts of fourteen films, winning an Oscar nomination for *Skippy* (1931). But the film of that period with which he is most commonly associated is *Million Dollar Legs* (1932), coauthored with Henry Myers from a story that Joseph had written himself. *Million Dollar Legs*, a title that bears no relationship to the plot, was the kind of anarchic comedy—partly surreal, partly absurdist—at which the Marx Brothers excelled. But Edward Cline, who directed it, was neither Leo McCarey nor Sam Wood; and W. C. Fields (who was not at his best), Ben Turpin (who simply looked cross-eyed), and Jack Oakie (who looked bovinely rotund) were not the Marx Brothers. Nor was *Million Dollar Legs* another *A Night at the Opera* (1935). Joseph L. Mankiewicz could write beautifully crafted comedies but not lunatic farce. Apparently *Million Dollar Legs* was inspired by Joseph's memories of an Albanian pole-vaulter in the 1928 Olympics who wore goatskin shorts. Yet he did nothing with the poor athlete who might have become another Little Tramp. Instead Myers and Mankiewicz concocted a plot resembling an old burlesque sketch like "Crazy House" and set in the mythical third-world kingdom of Klopstokia, whose president (W. C. Fields) ends up winning the shotput by a fluke.

If Mankiewicz's presence can be felt in the film, it is in the verbal humor that consists of titles (the sign at Mata Machree's that reads "Not Responsible for Husbands Left Over Thirty Days"), wordplay (Fields's confusion of "ultimatum" and "tomato," "lizard" and "wizard," "bogeyman" and "buggy ride"), and double entendres (Jack Oakie: "I have it." Susan Fleming: "You don't look it"). Henry Myers suspects that Herman, the unbilled producer of *Legs*, wrote the opening title.[2]

Regardless, Myers and Mankiewicz were responsible for the opening title of their next collaboration, *Diplomaniacs* (1933), which was made at RKO and was based on a story that Joseph had written. From a comparison of the titles, it is clear that the team planned *Diplomaniacs* as the companion film to *Legs*: Opening title, *Million Dollar Legs:*"Klopstokia, a far-away country. Chief exports: goats and nuts. Chief imports: goats and nuts. Chief inhabitants: goats and nuts"; opening title, *Diplomaniacs*: "There are three important things we should know about the noble red man. The Indian never shaves because he has no beard. He has no left whisker and he has no right whisker."

As one might expect, *Diplomaniacs* imitated the loose structure and comic techniques of its predecessor, especially the verbal humor that ranged from satirical titles ("Geneva—where the nations of the world fight over peace") to bad puns ("Why do they call him Luke?" "Because he's not so hot"). It was varsity show humor that a true writer outgrows, as Joseph L. Mankiewicz did. Zaniness either mellows into pathos, as happened with the Marx Brothers in *Love Happy* (1949) where Harpo was almost Chaplinesque in his affection for Vera-Ellen; or else it grows tiresome as it does in the films of Mel Brooks. The so-called lunacy of *A Night at the Opera* is really controlled anarchy, while in *Diplomaniacs* the anarchy is undisguised bedlam that explodes into silliness when a bomb tossed into a peace conference leaves the delegates in blackface and white gloves, singing an antiwar song; and the silliness sinks into irresponsibility when the barber-buffoons (Bert Wheeler and Robert Woolsey) precipitate a world war into which they are drafted. One suspects *Diplomaniacs* was the college show Mankiewicz never wrote at Columbia.

A far better example of Mankiewicz's comic writing can be found in *If I Had a Million* (1932), an anthology film that was the work of seven directors and eighteen screenwriters. Mankiewicz supplied the frame narrative; collaborated on "The Three Marines" sketch; wrote the "Rollo and the Roadhogs" episode; and provided the stories for three others. In the film, a millionaire's decision to leave his money to total strangers provides the frame for the eight episodes that comprise the plot. The framing device shows the Joseph L. Mankiewicz with whom most audiences are familiar: the Mankiewicz who can reveal moral vacuity simply through an action such as a child's playing a recording of "I'll Be Glad When You're Dead, You Rascal, You" while the millionaire is supposedly breathing his last. The frame derives from the plot of Puccini's one-act opera, *Gianni Schicchi* (1918), which opens with the death of the wealthy Florentine, Buoso Donati, whose predatory relatives feign sorrow while the child of one of them plays marbles on the floor. In both the opera and the film, the plutocrat's family receives nothing. Mankiewicz would use the *Gianni Schicchi* motif again in *The Honey Pot* (1967), in which the dying millionaire was neither dying nor a millionaire.

Mankiewicz wrote the stories on which three episodes of *If I Had a Million* were based: "The China Shop," in which a much put-upon clerk in a china shop indulges in an orgy of crockery-breaking when he receives his million-dollar check; "The Streetwalker," in which a hooker uses her windfall to check into a deluxe hotel, stripping down to her pre-Code black lace bra and panties and slipping into bed, alone; and "The Forger," which disclosed, for the first time, Mankiewicz's penchant for the perversely tragic, prefiguring the irony of the doomed marriage between a sensuous woman and an impotent man in *The Barefoot Contessa* (1954) and destiny's cruel hoax of a rattlesnake's leaping out of a pair of bloomers that a robber thought was stuffed with money in *There Was a Crooked Man* (1970).

In "The Forger," the title character, unable to cash his check, exchanges it for a ten-cent bed in a flop house while the owner, thinking the check is worthless, uses it to light his cigar. "The Three Marines" reverses the plot-switch of "The Forger" but without loss of irony. A marine, anxious to have a date with a waitress, gives his check, which he also thinks is phony, to her illiterate employer, convincing him it is really for ten dollars.

The most popular episode in the film is Mankiewicz's "Rollo and the Roadhogs," in which two ex-vaudevillians, played by W. C. Fields and Alison Skipworth, use their million to open up a tea shop. When a roadhog wrecks their car, they buy a fleet of jalopies and form an antiroadhog brigade. "Roadhogs" was an early portrait of the paradoxical Mankiewicz, the sentimental nasty (somewhat like Fields himself), who could treat Fields and Skipworth as if they were comic royalty yet put them in a situation requiring them to be vindictive and, at the same time, positively funny. It takes a rare talent to portray revenge without reducing it to pettiness. Comic destruction, while sanctioned by antiquity, is difficult to achieve; Mankiewicz achieved it in "Roadhogs" by giving it a human context, as he did the bitchiness in *All about Eve* (1950) and the games-playing in *Sleuth* (1972).

Mankiewicz has never been much for self-quotation, but occasionally he tosses in a reference to Wilkes-Barre, his birthplace, notably in *All about Eve.* Bette Davis recalls doing a play in Wilkes-Barre that contained a line about "the evil that men do." The play is Shakespeare's *Julius Caesar,* and Davis is misquoting Antony's Funeral Oration as Gary Merrill reminds her: "You've got it wrong. Even for Wilkes-Barre." In "Roadhogs," a friend is trying to remember when she and Skipworth last worked together. "Was it Wilkes-Barre, in '24?" she asks. "'23, dear," Skipworth replies.

The Lion Roars

The opportunity to work on the screenplay of *Manhattan Melodrama* (1934) brought Mankiewicz to MGM. The film involved at least three other writers including Oliver H. P. Garrett, Rowland Brown, and Pete Smith. The theme of *Manhattan Melodrama,* boyhood friends who ended up on opposite sides of the law, was repeated in such films as *Angels with Dirty Faces* (1938) and *Cry of the City* (1948). But what is historically significant about the movie, which won Arthur Caesar an Academy Award for best original story, is its connection with John Dillinger. On 22 September 1934 Dillinger was killed when he was leaving Chicago's Biograph Theater with the "woman in red" after they had seen *Manhattan Melodrama,* which ended with Clark Gable smiling on his way to the electric chair.

After writing the screenplays of *Forsaking All Others* (1934) and *I Live My Life* (1935) for MGM, Mankiewicz realized he wanted to direct his own work. But MGM was essentially a producer's studio, and he had to settle for producing. Mankiewicz no sooner embarked on this new phase of filmmaking than he began evidencing a quality that has always been associated with creative producers like David O. Selznick, Darryl F. Zanuck, and Hal B. Wallis: he supervised each film, refusing to be intimidated by the credentials of the screenwriter or the director. At Fox, Zanuck would behave similarly to Mankiewicz. But just as Zanuck's judgments generally proved sound, so did Mankiewicz's. It did not bother him to tone down Fritz Lang's expressionism in *Fury* (1936), despite Lang's European reputation. Humility was not one of Mankiewicz's virtues. Nor did he believe in coddling novelists who could not adjust to screenwriting. He simply rewrote their scripts, as he did F. Scott Fitzgerald's *Three Comrades* (1938), an action that prompted one of the most pathetic defenses a writer ever made: "Oh, Joe, can't a producer ever be wrong? I'm a good writer—honest." Fitzgerald was an excellent writer, but not of screenplays. While Mankiewicz could not have written *The Great Gatsby,* he could have adapted it; but Fitzgerald could adapt neither his work nor anyone else's. After checking Mankiewicz's revisions against the shooting script, Gore Vidal concluded that less than one third of Fitzgerald's dialogue for *Three Comrades* reached the screen; and that Mankiewicz's changes, which included the addition of the anti-Nazi subplot, at least resulted in dialogue that the actors could speak.[3]

The way Mankiewicz handled Fitzgerald's screenplay of *Three Comrades* anticipated his method of dealing with scripts he found unfilmable in their original form—for example, *Five Fingers* (1952) and *Cleopatra* (1963). He reworked them until he managed to produce a written template of what the film would ultimately be. No doubt, Mankiewicz contributed to each of the nineteen films he produced during his tenure at MGM. Since he has not enumerated all of his contributions, one would have to use reverse comparison to isolate them, working backward from his later work to his MGM period to find points of similarity. Obviously, the decade he spent at MGM had some influence on the films he made at Twentieth Century-Fox. In one instance, Mankiewicz has made it possible for us to see exactly how that influence operates. He has admitted that the stop-action ending of *The Philadelphia Story* (1940) was his inspiration. In fact, he takes a certain pride in having introduced a freeze-frame ending two decades before Truffaut made it into a cinematic commonplace with *The Four Hundred Blows* (1959). Clearly, then, the shot in *All about Eve*, when Mank stop-framed as Eve was about to receive the Sarah Siddons award, was not a Mankiewicz first. Nor, for that matter, was the freeze in *The Philadelphia Story*. Mankiewicz may not remember, but stop action was used in the second film he produced at MGM, *Fury*. Whether it was his idea or Fritz Lang's is unknown. At any rate, in the courtroom sequence the witnesses who denied their participation in the burning down of a jail, by claiming that they were elsewhere at the time, are shown a film of the event that proves they are lying. In a series of stop-action shots, they are seen throwing firebrands or breaking into the jail.

The sophisticated comedies Mankiewicz produced at MGM—*Double Wedding* (1937), *The Philadelphia Story*, *The Feminine Touch* (1941), *Woman of the Year* (1942)—were the link between the madcap farce of *Million Dollar Legs* and *Diplomaniacs* and the urbanity of *A Letter to Three Wives* (1949), *All about Eve*, and *People Will Talk* (1951). When one realizes that Mankiewicz produced *Fury*, a frightening study of mob violence, *No Way Out* (1950), which portrayed violence on the racial level, seems less atypical. Similarly, the social-climbing Lora May of *A Letter to Three Wives* is not a new breed in Mankiewicz's work; her precursor was Jessie (Joan Crawford) in *Mannequin* (1937), Mankiewicz's seventh MGM film. Lora May's tough veneer and "What's it to you?" attitude also were embodied in another Joan Crawford character (Julie) in *Strange Cargo* (1940).

Mankiewicz's ability to impart a vulnerable quality to actresses like Linda Darnell, Bette Davis, and Ava Gardner, whose screen personae militated against vulnerability, was prefigured in *Woman of the Year*, one of the last films he produced at MGM. Dissatisfied with Ring Lardner, Jr.'s and Michael Kanin's ending, he devised his own. Rather than allow Tess Harding (Katharine Hepburn) to maintain her aura of infallibility, he revealed her as a complete failure in the kitchen when she was unable to make breakfast for Sam Craig (Spencer Tracy). Had

Mankiewicz directed *Woman of the Year* instead of George Stevens, Tess's lack of domesticity might have been touching as well as laughable; at least it was human. Hepburn needed George Cukor to bring out the woman behind the mask, although it is quite possible that Mankiewicz could have done it as well.

The Spotlight Summons

It was inevitable that Mankiewicz would spend his most creative period (1943–51) at Twentieth Century-Fox. As Philip Dunne has observed, Darryl F. Zanuck, then vice-president in charge of production at Fox, "built up from the script rather than down from the star"[4] because, like Samuel Goldwyn, who also emphasized the script because he had comparatively few stars, Zanuck knew that the Fox pantheon could not compete with MGM's "more stars than are in heaven." As a former writer, even though he only wrote pulp fiction, Zanuck had more respect for the written word than Louis B. Mayer. Furthermore, even if Mayer had given Mankiewicz the chance to direct at MGM, it is questionable that he could have achieved the same measure of success as he did at Fox. George Cukor was MGM's resident *literatus*; whether there would have been room for another is doubtful. Besides, Mankiewicz and MGM were not aesthetically compatible. There was something about the typical MGM product that reminded one of a gourmet meal served cafeteria style; such was the alliance of Irving Thalberg's grand bourgeois style and Mayer's chicken soup ethic. The MGM logo had a lion roaring out of a wreath inscribed with *Ars Gratia Artis*, "Art for Art's Sake," a motto that was not only pretentious and inaccurate but bad Latin as well; *Ars Artis Gratia* was better Latin. The Fox logo, on the other hand, was imposing but unaffected: the studio's name in three-dimensional letters spotlighted by crisscrossing beams with a flourish of trumpets and drums.

In 1943, when Mayer's autocratic paternalism became overbearing, Mankiewicz parted company with MGM. Luckily, Fox came through with a five-year contract that allowed him to write, produce, and direct. Having progressed from Paramount Pictures on Marathon Street in Hollywood to MGM in Culver City, Mankiewicz moved on to Fox in Beverly Hills.

For his first Fox assignment, Mankiewicz chose to produce the screen version of A. J. Cronin's 1941 novel, *The Keys of the Kingdom*, which chronicled the life of a Catholic missionary. His decision to produce a religious film is not all that surprising when one remembers that he also produced *Strange Cargo* at MGM, one of the first movies to feature a genuine Christ figure and a film that Mankiewicz still respects. Significantly, he did not produce any other film during his eight-year association with Fox once he realized that Fox, unlike MGM, was a studio of directors and writers, but not producers.

Mankiewicz did more than produce *Keys*; he took over the script from Nunnally Johnson, who was leaving Fox—although he returned six years later. Johnson had written an adaptation that Zanuck deemed "unsatisfactory."[5] Zanuck then turned the screenplay over to Mankiewicz who rewrote it, claiming sole screen credit. However, when the matter went to arbitration, the Screen Writers Guild decided on co-credit with Mankiewicz's name preceding Johnson's.

The Significance of *The Keys of the Kingdom* (1944)

The Keys of the Kingdom occupies a special place in Mankiewicz's career because it illustrates his mastery of two of the most common, and therefore most abused, techniques in film: flashback and voiceover narration. If one compares this film with Mankiewicz's others using flashback, it becomes clear that its narrative structure served as the model for such movies as *A Letter to Three Wives, All about Eve,* and

Rosa Stradner (the second Mrs. Joseph L. Mankiewicz) and Gregory Peck as Mother Maria-Veronica and Father Chisholm in The Keys of the Kingdom. *(Credit: Margaret Herrick Library)*

The Barefoot Contessa. Mankiewicz understood that when flashbacks comprise the bulk of a film, narrative importance determines how long or short a flashback will be. Thus, he divided the flashbacks into units of varying length so that the narrative burden was not shared equally but rhythmically, with the segments balancing and complementing each other. Although filmmakers have perennially used flashbacks, few have learned, as Mankiewicz has, that flashbacks must be variegated and motivated; that some require voice-over and titles while others need only voice-over.

Essentially, the technique was the literary flashback adapted to film where voice-over replaced first-person narration, with the rhythm deriving from segmentation of details rather than their uninterrupted accumulation. Like Cronin's novel, the film was the dramatization of the journal of Father Francis Chisholm (Gregory Peck), who was being investigated for preaching "advanced" sermons and admitting publicly that all atheists are not godless. For the flashbacks to be plausible, someone must discover the journal. When Chisholm retires for the evening, Monsignor Sleeth (Cedric Hardwicke), who has been sent by the bishop to determine whether Chisholm is capable of serving his parishioners, comes upon the journal and begins perusing it. The reading of the journal determined the film's form—flashbacks with voice-over narration. For variety, the flashbacks were broken up into narrative units that were properly spaced; for diversity, Sleeth's voice was sometimes synchronized with the text, so that the audience heard him reading the words they saw on the screen. At other times, Sleeth's voice was heard alone, without the corresponding insert.

Sleeth's reading of the journal also created a framing device for the flashbacks, a technique Cronin had used in the novel. However, the frame is in turn "framed" by opening and end titles. The result is an eleven-part flashback with a frame narrative that begins and ends with a text—the opening title serving as a preface, the end title as an epilogue: (A) opening title: "On a September evening in 1938, Father Francis Chisholm returned to his little church near Tweedside, Scotland"; (B) frame narrative (I): Monsignor Sleeth's arrival; (C) flashbacks (1878–1938): (1) insert of journal entry read by Sleeth in voice-over narration; Francis's boyhood and his parents' death; (2) insert + voice-over; Francis's manhood and his departure for college; (3) voice-over without insert, as Sleeth's voice is heard reading Francis's candid assessment of his scholastic abilities; (4) insert + voice-over without dramatization; Francis's admission of his initial failures as a priest which are narrated, not visualized; (5) insert + voice-over; Francis's arrival in China; (6) insert + voice-over; establishment of mission; (7) insert + voice-over; passage of two years and arrival of nuns; (8) voice-over without insert;

Francis's frustration at his inability to win reverend mother's friendship; (9) voice-over only; arrival of Angus Mealy; (10) voice-over without insert; passage of ten years; (11) voice-over without insert; the fruits of Francis's priesthood; (D) frame narrative (II): Sleeth's decision that Francis remain in his parish; (E) end title. "And I will give to thee the keys of the kingdom of heaven"—Christ to Peter.

After Mankiewicz saw *The Keys of the Kingdom* on the screen, he resolved to direct his next film. He felt, somewhat unfairly, that John M. Stahl's direction of the film was inadequate to his script. The truth is that Stahl directed *The Keys of the Kingdom* in a workmanlike fashion but without the poetic intensity that Henry King infused into *The Song of Bernadette* (1943). As a result, *The Keys of the Kingdom* was more inspirational than spiritual; it lacked a director whose faith in the theme matched that of his protagonist, a shortcoming that might explain why so few films on religious subjects have been works of art.

Within a year, Mankiewicz would be sitting in the director's chair; but the hoped-for masterpiece was still in the future.

2

Perverse Patroons and Tinkering Tailors

A DIRECTOR'S first film can have everything, little, or nothing to do with his later work. It can be distinctive or anonymous, prefigurative or atypical; it can be a seminal film or merely apprentice work. Mankiewicz had been in the industry for seventeen years before he directed his first film, having already distinguished himself as an Oscar-nominated screenwriter and an MGM producer. Thus one expected a directorial debut that was promising, if not spectacular; *Dragonwyck* was neither.

Dragonwyck (1946)

One wishes that *Dragonwyck*, Mankiewicz's adaptation of Anya Seyton's 1944 novel of the same name, had been better so it could have been the successor to *Gaslight* (1944), the paradigm of the film of conjugal terror. The novel had all the elements: a gothic mansion on the Hudson, an ancestral curse, ethereal harpsichord music emanating from the Red Room, and a Nietzschean husband so obsessed with siring a male offspring that he poisoned his first wife when she could not bear him a son and planned a similar fate for his second when the son she bore him died.

The novel was an historical romance with gothic overtones as distinct from a gothic novel with an historical setting. The maiden's initiation into a world of evil was set against the background of the antirent movement of the 1840s in which the tenant farmers of the Hudson Valley estates rebelled against the inequities of the patroon system that reduced them to the level of serfs while elevating the patroon to the rank of manor lord. Seyton seems to have envisioned a novel in which the social history of the period would generate the narrative whose events would in some way reflect the struggle between the forces of tyranny and

John Hodiak and Nancy Guild in Somewhere in the Night.
(Credit: Margaret Herrick Library) 31

self-determination. While her purpose was laudable, the execution was disappointing. History became the servant of fiction rather than its equal.

However, Fox purchased *Dragonwyck* in 1943 when it was still being serialized in *Ladies' Home Journal*. Mankiewicz did not think much of Fox's new acquisition. When he was asked to rate its screen potential, he wrote that there was "less . . . than meets the eye," calling Seyton's knowledge of politics "naive, oversimple." Yet he begrudgingly admitted that "the opportunities for production values are exciting." Mankiewicz was so eager to direct a film that he became the victim of his own critique when Ernst Lubitsch chose him as *Dragonwyck*'s director.

With Lubitsch producing, Mankiewicz now thought the project might succeed. However, Lubitsch, who had come to Fox in 1943, was in notoriously poor health and died of a heart ailment a year after *Dragonwyck* was released. Although Mankiewicz initially thought it would be instructive to work with the creator of the Lubitsch touch, the creator withheld it, and the conflict between the men caused Lubitsch to remove his name as well. No producer's name appears in the credits which conclude with "Written for the Screen and Directed by Joseph L. Mankiewicz."

Part of the problem with *Dragonwyck* can be traced to the physical production. It needed something between the gilt of *Forever Amber* (1947) and the artificial opulence of *A Royal Scandal* (1945); instead it was given the best-seller look of *The Foxes of Harrow* (1947). Even the credits appeared against a Dragonwyck sketch that resembled a dust jacket.

But the main difficulty was the novel itself. Mankiewicz had two choices in adapting it: he could emphasize the gothic elements (gloomy mansion, lunatic husband, terrorized wife), minimizing or deleting the social and ideological ones; or he could make the clash of the classes (patroon and tenant farmers) and their respective ideologies (autocracy/democracy) the film's axis, weaving the gothic strands around it. Mankiewicz did both; the gothic lost, democracy won.

There is a democratic aura about *Dragonwyck* that, to some extent, recalls *Citizen Kane* (scripted by Mankiewicz's brother Herman). In fact, both films proceed from the same premise: the low-born child who is allowed to enter the world of the American aristocrat and enjoy the opportunities denied to the members of his or her class. *Dragonwyck* opens, as the novel does, with Abigail Wells (Anne Revere) receiving a letter from her cousin, the patroon Nicholas Van Ryn (Vincent Price), inviting her to send one of her daughters to Dragonwyck, his Hudson Valley estate, where the lucky girl might "enjoy the many advantages which she could not hope to enjoy in her present situation." In *Citizen*

Kane, those "advantages" consisted of Charles Foster Kane's enrolling in the best colleges in the country and getting expelled from each; running a newspaper; flirting with politics; building an opera house to showcase his monumentally untalented wife; and dying in the cold splendor of Xanadu. In *Dragonwyck*, Miranda Wells (Gene Tierney) is accorded the privilege of seeing medieval feudalism operating on the Hudson, living in a cursed mansion, marrying a mad husband, and narrowly escaping death at his hands.

Visually, the opening scenes also recall *Kane*, particularly in the way light and darkness are contrasted. In *Kane*, Orson Welles created a sharp contrast between the snow-covered yard where the young Charles was playing and the dark, austere interior of his mother's boardinghouse where his future was being sealed. Similarly, in *Dragonwyck*, the Wells farmhouse is stark and uninviting, its ceiling low and oppressive; the countryside, on the other hand, is impressionistically bright. There was also a physical resemblance between Agnes Moorhead, who played Mary Kane, and Anne Revere.

It is not surprising that Mankiewicz used motifs from *Kane* since his brother had written it; it was also a screenplay that Mankiewicz admired. One wishes *Dragonwyck* were another *Kane*. But Miranda Wells is a melodramatic heroine, not a tragic figure; and *Dragonwyck* is not American myth but historical romance with gothic trappings. The historical framework, such as it was, enabled Seyton—and Mankiewicz—to provide an egalitarian contrast to the mad patroon: Dr. Jeff Turner (Glenn Langan) who supports the farmers in their struggle for self-determination. But he also functions as the traditional deliverer; in the thriller, the heroine is usually saved by a kindly police inspector or a high-minded male who waits until her husband has been apprehended before declaring his love. Turner was the latter, and although everything pointed to Miranda's becoming his wife, Mankiewicz was requested to add an epilogue belaboring the obvious.

Mankiewicz planned an ending quite different from the novel's. Instead of dying a hero's death as he does in the original, Van Ryn would be shot by one of his tenant farmers and die in the thronelike rent chair. By having some of the farmers respectfully doff their hats, Mankiewicz would suggest that even in death the archetypal villain could inspire awe. "That's right," the dying Van Ryn sneers. "Take off your hats in the presence of the patroon."

It would have been an effective fadeout, with the camera slowly tracking back. As it happened, it became an effective lead-in to an ineffective epilogue similar to the one that closed out the novel. Thus novel and film end the same way, with Jeff's asking Miranda when he may call on her.

Anyone would find it difficult to carpet Seyton's rickety plot. Perhaps Hitchcock could have muffled the creaking, but Mankiewicz increased it with dialogue that was archaically epigrammatic ("Deformed bodies depress me," Van Ryn yawns) or unsuitably glib. A line like "I'm happy you're happy" is lost in *Dragonwyck*; when Bette Davis delivers it in *All about Eve*, it is memorable. Furthermore, the performances were uninspired except for Gene Tierney's Miranda. Price was hammy; Langan, colorless. Van Ryn's use of a Persian oleander to do away with his wife was intriguing, but in the film the way the plant caused death was never satisfactorily explained. One might infer it was through the leaves, one of which Price plucked dramatically while noting "how alive it is, as if it had a mind of its own." In the novel, Van Ryn ground the leaves in a nutmeg mill and sprinkled them on his wife's rum cake; in the film, one learns that the plant is a "glucoside similar in action to digitalis but more toxic," which, to the layman, is like explaining the nature of a product by rattling off its ingredients.

Dragonwyck was Mankiewicz's only flirtation with the gothic; he would never again yield to its blandishments. Hierarchically, the gothic is a lesser form of the romance; Mankiewicz excelled in the higher form of a genre. Still, *Dragonwyck* is worthy of discussion because it embodies a theme that became Mankiewicz's trademark: class conscious-

Vincent Price, Gene Tierney, and the fatal oleander in Dragonwyck. (*Credit: Margaret Herrick Library*)

ness, which is so universal that it transcends gender, profession, and time. The Mankiewicz commoner can be male or female; so can the Mankiewicz aristocrat. Class conflict can occur between members of the same sex or the opposite sex. Occupation and race are irrelevant. Aristocrats can be bluebloods, snobs, nouveaux riches, or white racists.

To bring the class theme forward from the background to which Seyton had relegated it, Mankiewicz emphasized Miranda's spunkiness, making her the first of a series of free-thinking women who had little patience with pretense. For this reason, he intensified the encounter between Miranda and the local virgins at the ball, which took place in the fifth chapter of the novel, so that it became a test of Miranda's mettle. Throughout the scene, Mankiewicz used a running gag; whenever one of the virgins would call her "Miss Van Wells," Miranda would answer, "Just plain Wells."

Miranda is also addicted to exclaiming "Golly Moses!" which is another Mankiewicz touch. Theatergoers will remember it as Tracy Lord's favorite expression in Philip Barry's *The Philadelphia Story* (1939), the movie version of which Mankiewicz produced at MGM. To Mankiewicz, a Philadelphia Main Liner and a Connecticut farm girl can register awe in the same way.

Although Mankiewicz did not find his metier in *Dragonwyck*, he discovered a subject that interested him and a character type he could develop. If he had a vehicle worthy of the subject and a plot that allowed for depth of characterization, he might have made a better film. Since it was his first film, one can excuse the spatial awkwardness of some of the scenes in which the characters were too far away to overhear or react as they did. The scene in which Van Ryn boldly danced with Miranda in the presence of his wife and guests needed the daring and abandon that Vincente Minnelli gave the waltz in *Madame Bovary* (1949). And some of the shots were a trifle self-conscious, especially the one of Turner and Van Ryn confronting each other in profile as Miranda enters the frame. A similar composition works better in *House of Strangers* (1949) when two bank guards face each other as Richard Conte enters the frame from the back.

Basically, Mankiewicz did not understand that one improves hokum like *Dragonwyck* by making it appear better than it is, as Hitchcock constantly did with material that, without his art, would have been mediocre melodrama. If one cannot produce a first-class screenplay from a second-rate novel, then the film must be given a superior visual style to compensate for the script and distract the audience's attention from inconsistencies and lapses of logic. Adaptation is not an act of reciprocity; a gothic novel does not automatically translate into a gothic film. In most cases, gothic material must be embellished with a style so fluid that audiences think it is poetic. Mankiewicz's mistake was to follow the classical principle of propriety and fit the style to the script. His theory of filmmaking is remarkably similar to Hamlet's theory of performance: "Suit the action to the word, the word to the action; with this special observance, that you o'erstep not the modesty of nature." In *Dragonwyck*, Mankiewicz gave an undistinguished story an undistinguished treatment.

Somewhere in the Night (1946)

Mankiewicz fared somewhat better with his second film, *Somewhere in the Night*, which at least challenged his abilities as a screenwriter and allowed him to experiment with subjective camera. While Zanuck was in Europe, Anderson Lawler came upon Marvin Borowsky's story, "The Lonely Journey," that impressed him enough to want to produce the movie version. Lawler showed the story to Somerset Maugham, who was in Hollywood in 1945. Maugham agreed that it had potential and even offered suggestions. Lawler then approached Mankiewicz, who was eager to direct another film even if it meant another melodrama. When Zanuck returned to Hollywood, the screenplay was ready, supposedly coauthored by Mankiewicz and Howard Dimsdale, but actually more by Mankiewicz than Dimsdale.

Somewhere in the Night is a film about amnesia, a type not uncommon in the 1940s that brought forth *I Love You Again* (1940), *Random Harvest* (1942), *Spellbound* (1945), *Identity Unknown* (1945), *Two O'Clock Courage* (1945), and *Love Letters* (1945). The plot involves a marine whose memory had vanished when a grenade had exploded in his face in the South Pacific. It has a small group of admirers who insist on calling it *film noir* which, superficially, it is; the credits appear against a dark sky dotted with swirls of cloud; the streets look tar-papered; the night is inky; the lighting is low key; the bars are smoky and menacing; the hotels have long dark corridors. However, *Somewhere in the Night* is more thriller than *noir*; the intricacy of its plot recalls *The Big Sleep* (1946), but unlike the Howard Hawks film, *Somewhere in the Night* is not much fun because it takes itself seriously. Mankiewicz did not know how to kid his material as Hawks did, nor did he have stars with the parodistic abilities of Humphrey Bogart and Lauren Bacall; he had only John Hodiak, on loan from MGM, as George Taylor and Nancy Guild in her screen debut as Christy.

There is, however one consolation: *Somewhere in the Night* might have been even more turgid had not Zanuck, in a 7 November 1945 memo, requested specific deletions. Mankiewicz, who has a fund of medical knowledge dating back to his Columbia days when he toyed with the possibility of psychiatry, included too many references to the plastic surgery that was done on the marine's face. Zanuck wanted them removed along with the opening scene in which a Japanese soldier, feigning surrender, hurled a grenade into a troop of marines. Zanuck was right; this was not a war film and should not begin as one. Interestingly, Zanuck objected to the obviousness of one of Christy's lines: "He [Lieutenant Kendall] knows everything. I'll bet he knows about my appendicitis scar." Zanuck must have felt that Mankiewicz, who prided himself on his wit, needed an occasional reminder that every line he wrote was not Wildesque: "Now really, Mr. Mankiewicz, you'll find something bright and clever to take the place of this corny line, won't you?" Zanuck also wanted two less murders; Mankiewicz had overdone it by killing off the moll and Phillips, the villain (Richard Conte). It is easy to forget that Phillips, although shot at the end, is not going to die since Kendall's announcement that he will recover is a throwaway line. Finally, Zanuck wanted a "smart and snappy line" to end the film. Here, Mankiewicz failed him.

Forced to provide a more imaginative beginning, Mankiewicz succeeded in coming up with one of the better examples of subjective camera at the same time that Robert Montgomery was shooting a whole film subjectively, *Lady in the Lake* (1946); and about a year before Delmer Daves did the same with the opening sequences of *Dark Passage* (1947). The first image that appears on the screen is a plasma bottle; then the camera tracks up to the bandaged face of the marine, George Taylor. Since he cannot speak, Mankiewicz uses extreme close-ups to express his reactions, voice-over narration to convey his thoughts, and subjective camera to denote disorientation. Interns face the lens when they discuss Taylor's case; a nurse peers into it when she tells Taylor to rap on the night table if he needs anything. The patient is the camera, and the audience becomes the patient, spoken to directly from the screen.

Discharged without a memory but with a new face, Taylor embarks on the perennial quest for identity. Destiny cooperates by blazing a trail of objects and events that lead him to the knowledge he is seeking. Learning that his last civilian address was a Los Angeles hotel, he checks in and examines the register. There is no record of a George W. Taylor, but there is one of a Howard Koch. Ordinarily, Mankiewicz avoids name-dropping and paying *hommage* to movie greats. Presumably he needed a name for the register since it is doubtful that a 1946 moviegoer would know that Howard Koch was the eminent screenwriter responsible for such films as *The Letter* (1940), *Sergeant York* (1941), and *Casablanca* (1942).

Taylor's footlocker contains a baggage check which yields a briefcase with a gun and a note on Elite Baths stationery signed "Your pal, Larry

Cravat" and informing him that $5,000 has been deposited in his name at a local bank. However, the bank teller becomes edgy when Taylor inquires about the money, and the manager of the Elite Baths steers him to a night club where the threatening presence of two thugs prompts him to take refuge in Christy's dressing room where he spots a postcard on which is written, "By the time you get this I'll be Mrs. Larry Cravat. Mary."

If one feels that the plot has thickened but is nowhere near boiling, it is because Mankiewicz has filled it with so many ingredients that it can only simmer. Part of the pleasure of watching a thriller is a willing suspension of disbelief and a refusal to hold the filmmaker responsible for the inevitable breakdown of logic. But in *Somewhere in the Night*, logic does not break down; it doggedly persists. *The Big Sleep*, on the other hand, makes sense until a black sedan is hauled out of the water at the Lido Pier; then the logic falls apart, but the real pleasure starts. In the thriller, plausibility is often a hindrance; one does not remember the plot, but only key scenes: Mary Astor's accusing Peter Lorre of attacking her in *The Maltese Falcon* (1941)—an allegation so ludicrous that it induces hysteria; Dorothy Malone's allowing Humphrey Bogart to seduce her (or was it the other way around?) in *The Big Sleep*. Mankiewicz repeats the conventions of the thriller, but he does it joylessly, as if he were following the rules.

Somewhere in the Night is a textbook thriller with all the stereotypes and motifs peculiar to the genre: the man on a search and the cool beauty who believes in him; the beauty's sympathetic boy friend who is really the villain; the avuncular cop who gets the last line; the moll who slinks into the hero's hotel room; the brutalization of the hero who, after getting the rubber hose treatment, awakens in an out-of-focus world like the widening gyre that greeted Dick Powell in *Murder, My Sweet* (1944); and trucks that run over men who know too much. Then there is the hardboiled dialogue with the outrageous metaphors and wacky conceits: "I've had more fun from drinking a Bromo-seltzer," Phyllis remarks when Taylor kisses her; Christy describes herself as the "girl with the cauliflower heart"; George's head spins like "a crazy squirrel on a hopped up treadmill." It is amazing what Mankiewicz can fit into 100 minutes; and these are only the conventions.

Now back to the plot which really does make sense—too much, in fact. Since Taylor knows that Larry Cravat holds the key to his identity, the film turns into a search for Cravat, an East coast private eye who, three years earlier, vanished without a trace along with two million dollars that had been floating around the country "like a pair of dice at a fireman's ball." Furthermore, Cravat is implicated in a dockside murder over the money that was witnessed by a workman named Conroy.

From a visit to the Conroy home, Taylor learns from Conroy's daughter, Elizabeth (Josephine Hutchinson), that her father is in a sanitorium. At this point, the action literally stops as Elizabeth delivers a poignant monologue on change: "And things change . . . but time doesn't change. Only people change. They grow old and ugly and pitiful." It is the most haunting moment in the film as Hutchinson bares her heart with ladylike reserve that, just when it seems on the verge of giving way to self-pity, is shored up by pride. It was as if Mankiewicz were tired of repeating conventions and tying more knots in the corded plot, and instead wanted to create a character with at least the semblance of flesh and blood. Elizabeth's monologue anticipates other Mankiewicz monologues—Eve's in *All about Eve,* Catherine's in *Suddenly, Last Summer* (1959), and especially Cecil Fox's ruminations on time in *The Honey Pot.*

Taylor goes to the sanitorium where he learns from the dying Conroy that there were four men on the dock that fatal night: Conroy himself, the murdered man, Cravat, and one other. Conroy also reveals that the money they were after is in a suitcase hidden under the dock between the pilings. And sure enough it is. But along with the two million is an old suit with an interesting label, to the effect that it had been tailored for Larry Cravat by W. George, Tailor. Thus Larry Cravat and George W. Taylor are the same person. Inspired by the label, Cravat changed his name to conceal his identity and joined the Marines to conceal his whereabouts.

Cravat now realizes he is a heel and a crooked shamus, but certainly not a murderer even though he was one of the unholy four. Then who was the fourth man? Phillips, whom Kendall plugs while offhandedly assuring the audience that he will live, presumably to stand trial so Cravat can start a new life with Christy.

Zanuck, one will remember, requested a "smart and snappy line" for the fade out. What Mankiewicz gave him was so banal that it almost reduced a well-constructed if uninspired film to a whodunit. Kendall, who is no Hercule Poirot, has an epiphany; now he knows why detectives keep their hats on in the movies: "If you want to shoot a man, you don't want to be holding a hat in your hand. It seems that the movies are right."

It was one of those hayseed endings, self-congratulatory and folksy, that was bound to induce a smile from those who could not follow the plot and a puzzled look from those who could. In a way, it was similar to the corny line or bit of business that often ended a Universal horror film.

What makes *Somewhere in the Night* different from the classic thriller is that the thriller keeps its innocence, no matter how corrupt the world is that it portrays. *Somewhere in the Night* bore the mark of experience;

it was too intelligent for its own good. Even the revelation is an elaborate pun: a suit tailored for a Cravat. The resolution was straight out of *Oedipus the King* where the searcher and the one for whom he is searching are the same person. Yet these details only succeeded in making the film more of a study in the art of the thriller than an expression of that art.

3

Three with Philip Dunne

MANKIEWICZ'S THIRD FILM, *The Late George Apley*, finally revealed his special gifts as a director. This was the first of three films that he directed from a Philip Dunne screenplay, the others being *The Ghost and Mrs. Muir* and *Escape*. Since a single intelligence seemed to be responsible for the screenplay and its visualization, one might assume that Mankiewicz had written *Apley* himself. Similarly, the screenplay of *Sleuth*, with its lancetlike dialogue, is so reminiscent of Mankiewicz that it is easy to forget that Anthony Schaffer, the author of the original play, did his own adaptation.

In the three films he made with Dunne, Mankiewicz was fortunate to have a screenwriter whose career paralleled his own and who could function as his alter ego. Both men had similar educational backgrounds: Mankiewicz was a graduate of Columbia; Dunne of Harvard. Mankiewicz entered the industry as a titler; Dunne as a script reader whom Fox hired at $35 a week in 1930, hoping to get a Harvard perspective on potential movie material. In 1932, Dunne moved from the old Fox studio on Western Avenue to MGM in Culver City as a junior reader, a year before Mankiewicz arrived there. In 1934, Dunne became a full-fledged writer with *The Count of Monte Cristo* which he coauthored with Rowland Lee, the same year MGM released *Manhattan Melodrama* which Mankiewicz coauthored with Oliver H. P. Garrett.

Like Mankiewicz, Dunne turned to directing, but later. Mankiewicz, who entered the industry in 1928, directed his first film in 1946; Dunne, who started in 1930, did not direct his first film, *Prince of Players*, until 1955.

Dunne was the ideal screenwriter for another reason: he believed that "direction is merely an extension of writing and there is but one concept when the writer-director do a picture together."[1] When Dunne began

Rex Harrison as the ghost of Captain Daniel Gregg in The Ghost and Mrs. Muir. *(Credit: Eddie Brandt's Saturday Matinee)*

43

directing, he simply considered himself "a writer who directs," as Mankiewicz did. Thus, when he was just a screenwriter, he was able to correlate his vision with the director's, so that by the time the film was made, the screenplay was inseparable from its realization.

The Late George Apley (1947)

The Late George Apley was such a film. Because of his Harvard background, Dunne was the logical choice to adapt John P. Marquand's story of a Boston aristocrat. However, there were two versions of *The Late George Apley*: the 1937 Pulitzer Prize novel spanning the period from Apley's birth in 1866 to his death in 1933 and consisting of letters to and from Apley along with some brief reminiscences by Apley himself; and the stage version with the same title, written by Marquand and George S. Kaufman and focusing on only one year in Apley's life—1912. The play, which starred Leo G. Carroll in the title role, opened on Broadway in November 1944 and enjoyed an 80-week run. Dunne wanted to incorporate material from the novel, but Zanuck insisted he concentrate on the play in which Apley is less of a stuffed shirt. Having spent $275,000 to acquire the screen rights, the highest Fox had ever paid at the time, Zanuck was unwilling to alienate audiences with a movie about an overbearing traditionalist. As it happened, Dunne humanized Apley so successfully that Marquand admitted that he preferred the film to the play.

Zanuck expected—and got—a quality film, if not an overwhelming success. *Apley* was too genteel, too civilized to win mass approval. Yet it was perfectly suited to Mankiewicz, who enjoyed plots about class consciousness, a subject he could treat without resorting to the rhetoric of exploitation. And how could Mankiewicz go wrong with a script in which the title character was a Boston blueblood able to acknowledge the existence of the Common but not of the commoner?

Perhaps because of its congenial theme, *Apley* allowed Mankiewicz to develop his own style as a director. But it was not a style that would evolve into a signature, or at least not into a discernible one. Rather, it would be his own kind of *mise-en-scène*—movie realism where the film acquires the lifelikeness of representational art and the wholeness of stage action without a stagy look. Mankiewicz's *mise-en-scène* was not limited to deep focus and long takes, although such techniques minimize the sense of fragmentation that comes from excessive cutting. Nor was his goal filmed theater in which the movie would resemble a play photographed from the stage like *New Faces* (1954) and *Top Banana* (1954). His goal was film as theater, film with the fluidity of stage action—a more difficult task to accomplish since one must use techniques like close-ups and medium shots that are alien to theater. For a film to achieve the organic wholeness of theater, it must proceed through several phases of integration, from the molding of the cast into an ensemble to the enmeshing of the ensemble with the physical production. The result seems felicitous because, while it can be described, it cannot be documented step by step. True *mise-en-scène* is creative energy transformed into meaningful work that leaves no trace of the effort that went into it.

Everything was right about *Apley,* starting with the credits that appeared against a succession of greeting card sketches of Boston. The camera was always the script's ally, matching the action but never competing with it and moving only when the occasion required. In the opening scene, George Apley (Ronald Colman), an inveterate bird watcher, hears the sound of a bird from a nearby tree as he is returning home. As he lifts his head, the camera looks up with him, tilting up to the branch and down to George, who is busy making an entry in his notebook. Even the celebrated 360-degree pan of the Apley clan that, according to an overly enthusiastic publicity release, was "the first time in motion picture history that a camera had been equipped to shoot a complete circle with no breaks,"[2] was not a display of virtuosity but a metaphor for the family circle that enfolds its own and excludes others.

There is a shot later in the film—one so unassuming that it can easily escape detection—that illustrates Mankiewicz's brand of realism. It occurs at Agnes's coming-out party and shows several couples sitting on the stairs of the Apley house; Mankiewicz will use a similar composition in *All about Eve* for the party scene. In 1945, when he was making *Dragonwyck,* Mankiewicz might not have considered such a group shot; or he might have fragmented it, by cutting from one character to the other. But in 1945, he was trapped in a gothic mansion; the Apley home on Beacon Street is more lifelike. It may be a soundstage home, but it looks like a real one with a staircase thronged by young couples eating cake and radiating an infectious vitality.

Mise-en-scène originates with the cast; when a performer is miscast, the entire production can suffer. A star ill suited to a role will also have problems with the costumes and set. *Apley* was cast according to type, with Britishers in the leads: Ronald Colman, Edna Best (Catherine), Richard Haydn (Horatio), Percy Waram (Roger), and the Anglo-Irish Peggy Cummins (Eleanor). They were not movie Britishers like C. Aubrey Smith and Dame Mae Whitty. They modified their accent to suggest New England rather than Great Britain, sounding no different from the Americans in the cast: Mildred Natwick (Amelia), Richard Ney (John), and the Austrian-born but UCLA-educated Vanessa Brown (Agnes).

Ronald Colman and Edna Best as George and Catherine Apley
in The Late George Apley. *(Credit: Margaret Herrick Library)*

There was nothing about Colman's George Apley to evoke the har-rumping patriarch. Colman was the perfect Apley because he was able to convey urbanity without seeming affected; hence his great success on radio in *The Halls of Ivy* (1950–52) in which he played Dr. William Todhunter of Ivy College. Colman might never have played the part had it not been for *Dragonwyck*. *Apley* was to mark his return to the screen after a two-year absence; the last film he made was the unmemorable *Kismet* (1944) at MGM. Since he was unfamiliar with Mankiewicz's work, he requested a screening of *Dragonwyck* before consenting to do *Apley*; he was obviously satisfied with what he saw.

Although George Apley was not an easy character to accept, audiences could at least respect him because Colman created a man whose words were not at variance with his actions. What might be reprehensible in one whose words belied his deeds was not in George, who is presented in the film as an Emersonian who has not yet embraced the consequences of Emersonianism. Emerson could accept human beings at their best and their worst; George could not, although what he considered their worst was hardly cause for alarm. He is shocked that his son John wants to marry a "foreigner"—his term for a non-Bostonian; he packs his daughter Eleanor off to Europe because she is in love with

Howard Boulder, a Harvard instructor, who dares to call Emerson, Hawthorne, and Melville the "Concord radicals." Apley is convinced that Howard is a radical and uses his influence to have him fired.

Yet George's actions are in character; one knows he will relent and that Eleanor and Howard will marry. For we are in the mythos of spring, as Northrop Frye called comedy in *Anatomy of Criticism*. Thus the patriarch will mellow; "a society controlled by habit, ritual bondage, arbitrary law and the older characters" will yield to one "controlled by youth and pragmatic freedom";[3] and the plot will terminate in the wedding or *gamos*—in this case, a double wedding, Eleanor and Howard, Agnes and John.

Dunne's screenplay never allows the audience to lose sight of the fact that the film is a comedy with social overtones as opposed to the novel, and to some extent the play, which were social satires with comic overtones. The screenplay also contains references to sex and virginity which, had they appeared in a different setting as they would several years later in *The Moon Is Blue* (1953), might have raised the hackles of the Breen Office and the Legion of Decency. However, no one took issue with them at the time because they were witty but innocent. When Eleanor argues that "coming out" is nothing but the old idea of "introducing the virgin to the rest of the tribe," her father replies, "We do not face virginity in the drawing room after a Thanksgiving dinner." In the same vein, George tries to explain Freud to his wife Catherine in terms of Emerson: "Dr. Freud is trying to do the same thing with sex—that Emerson did without it." When Catherine is amazed that anyone could write a whole book about sex, George is forced to admit that Freud seems "to pad it a little here and there."

In *Apley*, Dunne had to resolve a series of romantic entanglements caused by George's conservatism: Eleanor's love for the "radical" Howard, and John's attraction to the "foreign" Myrtle Dole. The only match George will sanction is the one he has proposed between John and Agnes; yet it seems hopeless because John considers his cousin plain and unattractive. While tradition requires the defeat of the obstructer or his conversion, verisimilitude demands a motivated defeat or a logical conversion. Therefore, the reversal is preceded by a scene creating sympathy for George, so that when his defeat comes, it will not be an occasion for gloating.

In the scene, Catherine Apley consoles Agnes by telling her the story of her husband's youthful infatuation with an Irish girl whom his father found socially inferior. To cure his lovesickness, George was sent on a tour of Europe. When he returned, he married the woman of his father's choice—his cousin who is, of course, Catherine. Since George has now been shown to be a man who has loved and lost, he seems considerably more human. Thus one does not cheer when he suffers what for him is a major defeat: failure to be elected president of the Blue Hill Bird Watchers' Society, whose members regard him as too narrow even for their taste.

If George were a true Emersonian, he would have considered the bird as a link in that "subtle chain of countless rings," as Emerson put it, that unites man with God; he would also have attempted to emulate the bird's distinctive feature: its ability to soar. It took a defeat to activate his Emersonianism and set him soaring. The defeat, then, was the means by which the *senex iratus* became the benign father.

As proof of his conversion, George agrees to a marriage between his son and Myrtle Dole. However, Myrtle's father, the owner of a prosperous tool and dye company, is unimpressed by George's plan to make the Doles acceptable to Boston society. Julian Dole needs neither Beacon Hill nor the Apleys; he also knows that Boston and Worcester are incompatible. The scene between the blueblood and the bourgeois makes its point with great subtlety: the bourgeoisie can be just as class-conscious as the aristocracy. The middle class also has the same solution for lovesick offspring—travel—although they send them to California, where Myrtle is headed, rather than Europe.

Realizing that Agnes's sexless appearance is what keeps John from seeing her as a potential wife, George whisks her off to New York for a transformation of her own. George's conversion is complete. He can now distinguish the accidents of tradition—its taboos and restrictions— from its essence—mores and values that have stood the test of time. Tradition may be sacred, but is accretions are often profane and, in turn, tend to profane tradition.

The title of the film has been vindicated, although not in the way Marquand originally intended. In the novel, George is dead from the beginning; in the play, there was an epilogue set in 1924, depicting John as a replica of George—a bird-fancier doting on his father's canary. In the film, George is very much alive at the end. Thus Rose Pelswick of the *Journal American* found the title confusing, as did the *Newsweek* critic.

Initially, the title was not meant to confuse. Less than three weeks before *Apley* went into production, the final script (dated 6 June 1946) called for the film to begin, as the novel did, with a reference to the literally late George Apley in the form of an opening title: "I am the sort of man I am, because environment prevented my being anything else—From the Papers of the Late George Apley of Beacon Street, Boston." The title was the last sentence of the novel's opening paragraph, unchanged. When it was decided that George would be alive throughout the film, the title was dropped and a simple insert—"Beacon Street Boston 1912"—added.

Yet there is a late George Apley in the film: the old George who bristled at the sight of a Grape Nuts sign overlooking the Common and who arranged his son's marriage as his father had arranged his. The new George sends Eleanor and Howard off to Europe with the boat tickets he had purchased for John and Agnes, telling them to marry on board.

The Late George Apley will never be considered a major film, nor is it one that automatically evokes the name of Joseph L. Mankiewicz. Yet it was the first film to show what Mankiewicz could achieve when he could use dialogue that was never less than civilized, even when it involved a discreet baring of the heart.

The Ghost and Mrs. Muir (1947)

Although *The Ghost and Mrs. Muir* opened at Radio City Music Hall, it was, like *Apley*, only a qualified success. Yet it is unique among Mankiewicz's films; it is a dreamscape, haunting and poetic, depicting the romance between a widow and the ghost of a sea captain. The 1945 novel by R. A. Dick (pseudonym of Josephine Aimee Campbell Leslie) was sprightly enough so that one never thought of the underlying theme—the romance of death, which appears more traditionally as the romantic fascination with the other world. Its ultimate expression is something like *Death Takes a Holiday*, Alberto Casella's play and Mitchell Leisen's 1934 film, in which Death is the lover and a mortal the beloved. More typical is the case of the lover from the other world (*Down to Earth*, 1947; *Portrait of Jennie*, 1948) or from another time (*Berkeley Square*, 1933; *Time after Time*, 1979). Then there are the comic dead or spirits whose conversations with the living lead outsiders to think that such mortals are daft (*Topper*, 1937; *For Heaven's Sake*, 1950). At one point, *The Ghost and Mrs. Muir* uses the *Topper* convention; when Lucy Muir (Gene Tierney) tells the ghost to "keep out of it," her in-laws take the reprimand personally.

While the film had its comic moments (some suggestive enough to merit a B rating, "Morally objectionable in part for all," from the Legion of Decency), it remained a love story even to the end when Captain Gregg (Rex Harrison) returned to bring his woman to his world. For at the end, love and death merged into a spiritual *Liebestod* as the couple found in eternity what they could not have on earth.

Films of this sort are always in danger of becoming cerebral, surreal, or expressionistic. Thus Dunne structured the screenplay linearly, with everything motivated from the outset. Lucy, a recent widow, refuses to live with her straitlaced in-laws and sets out upon a new life, bringing her daughter and faithful maid to a seaside village where she rents a house, Gull Cottage, supposedly haunted by the ghost of a sea captain. Just when one thinks the conventions of the haunted house movie will start operating—the ectoplasmic presence, creaking doors, sliding panels—Mankiewicz takes over, weaving visual poetry around Dunne's literate prose.

Oddly enough, it was John M. Stahl—not Mankiewicz—who was originally chosen for the film, on the basis of *Holy Matrimony* (1943)—the film version of Arnold Bennett's *Buried Alive*—which, for some reason, Zanuck thought qualified Stahl for *The Ghost and Mrs. Muir*. Here was a rare instance in which not only was Zanuck's choice of director wrong, but also his concept of the film. Zanuck, whose judgment was usually sound, contemplated another *Sentimental Journey* (1946) in which the dead Maureen O'Hara kept appearing to Natalie Wood. His choice for Lucy Muir was also bizarre: Norma Shearer who, as he observed in a memo (24 June 1946), "has one great picture left in her." By the time the film went before the cameras in November 1946, Mankiewicz was the director; and Dunne, who originally was to have collaborated on the screenplay with Fred Kohlmar, became the sole screenwriter, with Kohlmar producing.

Happily, Mankiewicz never carried out Zanuck's wishes, which, one assumes, changed before filming began. Yet Mankiewicz realized that the movie would have to live up to the audience's expectations. Since Gull Cottage was the prototypical haunted house, one expected an occasional *frisson*, which Mankiewicz was willing to provide, except that his *frissons* would be aesthetic. The audience can sense the ghost's presence even before Lucy's arrival at the cottage; a high shot of the car as it moves along the winding road suggests that someone is watching the new occupants. When Lucy inspects the bedroom, a lusty laugh rings out. These may be concessions to popular taste, but Mankiewicz conceded with more style and intelligence than one would ever find in the "old dark house" movies.

The director's vision sets *The Ghost and Mrs. Muir* apart from such movies. Mankiewicz saw more in the plot than a romance between a spirit and a mortal; he saw the romance of life and art (one short, the other long as the proverb goes) and the impossibility of their union, at least in this world. "Your life may be short, Madam. I have unlimited time at my disposal," the ghost tells Lucy. What she experiences in her short time with the captain is an introduction to the world of art and a preview of eternity. If the function of art is to transcend the ordinary and replace a brazen world with a golden one, as Sidney says, then Captain Gregg has shown her the realms of gold. By rescuing her from the mundane, he has given her the opportunity to become a heroine in a spectral romance, the sort that makes heroes and heroines out of mere men and women; tragic figures and star-crossed lovers out of ordinary mortals.

These were not points that could be made directly in the screenplay where they might seem pretentious or extraneous; but they can be made visually, aurally. Everything about the captain's world bears the stamp of art, including Bernard Herrmann's music that combines the lush impressionism of Debussy's *La Mer* with the seaswept starkness of the interludes from Benjamin Britten's *Peter Grimes*. Not only does Lucy enter another—as well as the other—world when she comes to Gull Cottage; she also enters a world where faces are portraits; nature, a seascape; and age, the gentle erosion of time.

The captain first appears as a face on a portrait that Lucy sees through an open door; Mankiewicz arranges that the ghost and Mrs. Muir, the painting and the woman, are in the same shot. He then cuts from this unusual two shot to a masked shot of the captain's face enshrouded in darkness. Significantly, when Captain Gregg appears in corporeal form, he looks exactly like his picture—a sea captain with an uncanny resemblance to Bernard Shaw. There are even times when Mrs. Muir looks like a figure on a canvas; dressed in her widow's weeds and lit in low key, she often looks not like Lucy Muir but like the Widow Muir—the subject and title of a painting. Being with the captain has given her the potential for acquiring the immutable form of perfection that is death's only gift.

Inevitably, the captain will make her his. "I've led a man's life," he boasts; he also confesses that he would escape to the crow's nest to read Keats. Thus one expects the ghostly consummation to be erotic, as befits one who has led a "man's life"; and tender, as befits one with a predilection for Keats. The taking of Lucy is a poetic act of spirit impinging on matter. While it is clearly not sexual, it is sensuous, to use D. H. Lawrence's distinction in *Women in Love* (1920). For sensuousness is all the captain has left.

The captain's first appearance is a triumph of pure directorial art, for it is completely without dialogue. As Lucy dozes off in an armchair, a gentle breeze blows open the terrace doors. The camera pans up to the clock above the mantel that has just struck 4:00 P.M.; then down to the dog on the window seat, over to the sleeping Lucy, and up again as the shadow of a man falls over her. The camera returns to the clock which registers a few minutes after the hour before dissolving to 5:00. Twilight has crept into the room, and Lucy is awakened by the banging doors. While she has been sleeping, the captain has made his spirit part of hers. But the truly memorable feature of the scene is that while the camera is not really subjective, it takes on the captain's sensuousness; it roams the room like a lover looking about and then moving toward his beloved, as the captain apparently did.

Lucy has not yet seen the intruder; nor have we, really. When we do, there will be some dialogue, but a bare minimum. For Mankiewicz is making a visual statement about art and reality by showing one, then the other. During a storm, Lucy opens the door to the sitting room, candle in hand and back to the camera. The light from the candle illuminates the face on the portrait; it also gives Lucy's black hair a silvery finish. Later that night, she sees the captain in the kitchen. Now she is not looking at the portrait, but at the man, however spectral he may be. This should be life, not art; yet there is no difference. The face she beholds is the face of the portrait. Art has become life, at least for a time. And, for a time, an ordinary kitchen becomes a painting in monochrome with bits of white subtly worked into a dark background: the steam from the kettle, Lucy's white nightgown, the light from the candle, and the lightning flashing against the window.

Since spirits neither marry nor give in marriage, their relationship with mortals can only be sensuously platonic. Yet a spirit and a mortal can collaborate, as the captain and Lucy do on a book—an autobiographical novel entitled *Blood and Swash*. The captain dictates, and Lucy transcribes. When she objects to typing a certain word, the captain defends it: "It's a perfectly good word." Lucy acquiesces and strikes four keys on the typewriter.

The book has an ambivalent effect on their relationship. First it brings them together; then it sets them apart. In her efforts to get the novel published, Lucy meets Miles Fairley (George Sanders), an author of children's books, whom the captain regards as a rival. Fairley, something of an artist, paints Lucy in a bathing suit, reducing a living portrait to pop art. In an especially touching scene, Mankiewicz brings Lucy, Fairley, and the captain into the same shot. When Fairley and Lucy kiss, the camera tracks back, revealing the captain behind a tree. He turns slowly and faces the camera before walking away and out of Lucy's life.

He leaves Lucy as he found her—asleep. His farewell is the opposite of his epiphany. This time, he does not bend over her like the storybook prince, ready to plant a kiss on the lips of the sleeping beauty. This time, the terrace doors do not bang; they close silently. This time, he speaks to the sleeping Lucy, telling her that everything they shared was a dream, except the book: "You wrote the book, you and no one else."

The captain has succeeded in convincing her it was a dream, but his departure has also made her more somnolent. She was asleep when his shadow passed over her; she was asleep when he left her. When she learns that Fairley is married, she sleeps again—through a montage of years. Mankiewicz repeats some of the same camera movements he had used when the captain entered her room: the ca era pans up to the clock, which again strikes 4:00 P.M.; then down to the dog and over to the French doors. But the camera has lost its sensuousness; now it imitates Lucy, not the captain. Too tired to repeat everything, the camera can only suggest what it had done before.

The years envelop each other like overlapping waves; gulls flying over the water dissolve into white caps. Lucy, a solitary figure, walks along the beach past the piling on which her daughter's name had been carved; the letters are already growing indistinct. After a bridging episode, more time passes; the piling lies on the beach, the letters virtually illegible. The seascape dissolves into a veranda where a white-haired woman is standing; it is the same veranda where the captain told Lucy that he used to read Keats. But the veranda is fogbound, and Lucy is old and frail. If her ghostly lover is to return, it should be now.

At Fox, a film could end with an apparition suggesting life after death without appearing to be pietistic. The end of *The Song of Bernadette*, in which the Virgin comes to take the dying Bernadette to paradise, could have been mawkish; at MGM, the two of them would have traipsed through the clouds. Yet, when Bernadette gazes at the Virgin and says, "I love you," one is genuinely moved. Less talented hands could have transmogrified *The Ghost and Mrs. Muir* into a supernatural weepie; Mankiewicz, Dunne, and Herrmann made it into a transcendent Love Death. Essentially, Lucy was in love with Death; it was a love that could only be satisfied in myth or in a dreamlike relationship with a visitor from death's kingdom. But mythic roles are difficult to sustain; dreams are evanescent; and art without an artist is impossible. To regain what she had with the captain, she must die.

Mankiewicz and Dunne do not rush Lucy's transfiguration. First she complains about a pain in her arm; then she reaches for a glass of milk, but it falls from her hand. Mankiewicz cuts to a knees-to-feet shot of Lucy, sitting in her chair; but another pair of legs—a man's—enters the frame. "You'll never be tired again. Come, Lucia. Come, me dear," a voice says. Finally, one sees the speaker, as the captain extends his hand to Lucy. But the woman rising from the chair is not a grandmother but the young Lucy, who leaves her corpse behind and joins her lover. Like a young couple, they walk down the stairs past the housekeeper. The door opens by itself, and the couple pass through it into eternity.

Mankiewicz has never made a film that was so richly poetic or one whose conventional veneer belies such depth. One wonders if Mankiewicz even knew he had created a work of art as well as a work about art. If he did, he might never have referred to himself as "the oldest whore on the beat." While whores are often subjects of art, they rarely produce it.

Escape (1948)

Philip Dunne adapted *Escape* from John Galsworthy's 1926 play of the same name; it was a play for which Dunne seems to have had a special affinity because of his sensitivity to Christian themes. In "Some Platitudes concerning Drama" (1909), Galsworthy argued that good plots come about from original sin, a term he used frequently in *Escape*. Galsworthy meant that fallen man, man at his most human, is the best subject for drama: "A human being is the best plot there is." Yet serious drama since the time of the Greeks has rarely left humankind in control of its destiny. The protagonist is always encountering the incalculable and the ineluctible. In *Escape*, Galsworthy attempted the difficult task of reconciling inexorable fate with Christian providence; by dramatizing the effects of original sin, he tried to show that the same nature that makes us the prey of fortune also makes us the wards of providence.

However, he was not dramatizing a simple case of bad luck. By coming to a prostitute's defense, Matt Denant has accidentally caused the death of the plainclothesman, who was apprehending her, and is sentenced to a three-year prison term. Morally, the issue is complex. The plainclothesman was doing his job, and Matt was putting his Christianity into practice by playing the Good Samaritan. Consequently, he made no attempt to flee when a policeman arrived. Yet Matt believes he was unjustly sentenced. Thus he escapes from prison; along the way he is aided by men and women who intuitively sense his innocence. Finally, he takes refuge in a church, thereby putting the parson in a position to practice his Christianity by giving a fugitive asylum. Rather than compromise the parson who hesitates when asked if he has seen the escaped convict, Matt surrenders.

If one had to reduce the play's theme to a single phrase, it would be original sin. In the prologue, the prostitute bitterly refers to herself as "original sin" in response to Matt's calling her "original." When asked what provoked the fight between himself and the plainclothesman, Matt replies: "God knows! Original sin." After he escapes, he enjoys a pleasant interval with an Old Gentleman that leaves both of them feeling more human. When the Old Gentleman tries to explain that feeling, he attributes it to "original sin."

The play was a Christian allegory with Matt as a Good Samaritan who stopped short of evolving into a Christ. Dunne completed the evolution by portraying Matt (Rex Harrison), now a former RAF squadron leader,

Rex Harrison as Matt Denant escaping in Escape. *(Courtesy: Twentieth-Century Fox)*

as the victim of injustice and betrayal. Accordingly, Dunne omitted Galsworthy's helpful proto-Christians and substituted bogus ones, the embodiments of unpurged original sin: a mean-spirited shopkeeper, a crooked car salesman, a friend who turns informer for the reward money.

Dunne invested the screenplay with a Graham Greene quality that was especially evident in the way he dramatized the paradoxes of Christianity, one of which is original sin. Dunne retained the conversation between Matt and the prostitute in which she dubbed herself original sin, as well as Matt's remark that original sin caused the entire incident. But Dunne did not stop there. He conflated two of Galsworthy's female characters—the lady who gave Matt her husband's Burberry and Dora, who did not disclose his presence to the constable—into one, Dora Winton (Peggy Cummins), who, in the tradition of the escape thriller, becomes Matt's companion as well as the film's love interest. It is she who now gives Matt the Burberry. When asked why, she replies, "I haven't the faintest idea." Matt suggests it might be original sin: "There seems to be an awful lot of it around." When Dora's sister asks a similar question, Dora gives original sin as the reason.

Matt knows all about original sin, having experienced it at its worst: self-righteousness, hostility, lovelessness. Yet in Dora and the parson he

encounters charity and benevolence which, paradoxically, are also effects of original sin—the primal sin, the sin of being born human instead
of divine. Original sin is double-edged; it destroys any chance of a
heaven-on-earth, yet it gives us our humanity—something a god cannot
possibly comprehend unless the god happens to be a man as well.
Original sin is the supreme paradox; as the first sin, it brings evil into the
world. But once one realizes this, salvation is possible, not by transcend-
ing human nature but by perfecting it. Ironically, the farmer who is bent
on turning Matt in thinks he has transcended it. When Matt cries in
desperation, "Haven't you got an ounce of original sin in you?" the
farmer answers that he is not a sinful man.

Although Dunne reproduced the substance of Galsworthy's plot, he
made major changes in the characters of Dora and the parson. A minor
figure in the play, Dora becomes one of Christianity's paradoxes—the
agnostic saint. Initially, Dora manifested the worst features of original
sin. Engaged to a man she does not love, she views marriage as a chance
to get her "share of the loaves and the fishes," misusing the New
Testament reference by making it a synonym for affluence. She also
thinks in terms of easy disjunctions—the haves and have-nots, the
hunter and the hunted. Significantly, Matt first sees her when she is
thrown from her horse during a fox hunt. Dora's imagery of the hunt
even offends her moralistic sister, who shudders when Dora rhapsodizes
about the "fine kill."

Yet when Dora meets Matt, she changes into the prototypical Christian who finds Christ in the outcast. In a masterpiece of subtle iconog-
raphy, Matt takes refuge in a ruined hut where Dora finds him lying in
the straw; as she takes him in her arms, they form a Pietà that inter-
weaves symbols of the Nativity and the Crucifixion with his suffering
becoming her rebirth.

At the end of the film, Dunne pushes paradox to its limit. Matt has
made Dora a better human being and, in turn, has become better
himself. Similarly, the parson will find the Christ in the criminal who
will, in turn, find humanity in the clergyman. Dunne's parson is more
articulate than Galsworthy's, speaking authoritatively about the city of
God and the city of man; and arguing that perfect justice is found only in
God and not in the church. Yet Dunne's parson, like Galsworthy's, also
hesitates when asked if he has seen Matt. Again Matt resolves the
parson's dilemma by giving himself up.

However, the parson realizes that Matt's case was an example of an act
of charity that backfired into tragedy; an act that derived from Matt's
"decent self," the self that tried to counteract original sin, only to come
face to face with it. Dunne adds a final scene, showing Matt returning to
prison, now purged of bitterness. Having encountered the unregener-

ate and the redeemed, he can accept them both; for both make up mankind. But it is the redeemed who balance the scales of justice that the unregenerate have upset. "That seems to be the trouble with all of us, doesn't it?" Matt says to the inspector at the fade-out. "Being human. I'd forgotten that."

Quotations from another Galsworthy play, *Justice* (1910), introduce and conclude the film: the opening title reads, "There is nothing more tragic in life than the utter impossibility of changing what you have done"; the end title, "The Law is what it is—a majestic edifice sheltering all of us, each stone of which rests on another."

Given the ironic title of the play from which they came, the quotations were peculiarly apt. Matt no more found perfect justice than the forger did in Galsworthy's earlier drama. But, as the parson cautioned, perfect justice does not exist on earth. What does exist here is love; and while love cannot alter the past, it can at least make it bearable. The end title is similarly ironic; the law in the film is not the monolith that the judge in *Justice* extols. Whatever majesty it has derives from a divine foundation that supports a human structure.

Although *Escape* seems to be atypical of Mankiewicz, it harks back to two films he produced at MGM—*Fury* and *Strange Cargo*. In the former, an innocent man, who is almost lynched, is consumed with misanthropy that only a woman's love can overcome; in the latter, a Christ figure effects the spiritual regeneration of a band of escaped convicts, even enabling them to accept death with resignation. Despite the fact that he disliked Dunne's screenplay, telling *Cahiers du Cinéma* that it was "a very bad adaptation" (which it was not), he directed it sympathetically. For the flashback, he used a simple metaphorical dissolve. The camera tracks up to Matt as he looks out of his prison window at a flock of birds that dissolves into a shot of Matt in a plane. The return to the past was done so imperceptibly that one scarcely noticed it was a flashback. Yet the flight image that connected past and present complemented the film's paradoxical design. To fly is to be free, but to be free, one must resort to flight. Dora reminds Matt that, by escaping, he is still enslaved, having exchanged one prison for another. Matt replies that by marrying a man she does not love, she will be exchanging one kind of poverty for another.

While paradox can prick the mind into action, it can elude moviegoers who prefer action of a less cerebral kind. Dunne attributed the film's failure in the United States to the inability of American audiences to understand British actors. One could well understand audiences having a problem since some of the actors had accents as thick as the fog through which Matt made his escape. However, the film's theology militated against its being a popular success. Thus Mankiewicz had to work harder to prevent the theology from impeding the action. Although he encountered technical problems during the filming, he maintained a realistic quality throughout—shooting on London streets, showing the crash of Matt's plane, and using mirrors and open windows as visual channels of information. For example, Matt enters Dora's house through an open window; she sees him in a bathroom mirror.

There is an aura of inexorability in *Escape* that is found in a good deal of *film noir*, especially in *They Won't Believe Me* (1947) and *Detour* (1945), which has the most blatantly fatalistic line in movie history: "Fate, or some mysterious force, can put the finger on you or me for no good reason at all." *Escape* offered a reason, but like everything else in the film, it was couched in paradox and might be summed up in the lesson of tragedy: learning through suffering. However, *Escape* is closer to Hitchcock than it is to *film noir*, especially to *I Confess* (1953) which also pushes a paradox—the seal of the confessional that prevents a priest's revealing a murderer's identity—to the limit. If audiences had difficulty with both films, it may be because they thought of original sin as an act committed in some ancient garden by two mythical people and not in their own time and by themselves.

4

A Missive for Madame

AT FIRST glance, *A Letter to Three Wives* and *The Honey Pot* seem to have little in common. The former was a triumph for Mankiewicz, winning Oscars in the categories of best screenplay and direction; the latter was a failure. However, the plot of each revolved around a letter sent to three women. In *Wives*, Addie Ross, the local gay divorcée, pens a note to three women, informing them that she has run off with one of their husbands. She does not write to each wife individually but sends one note flippantly addressed to the "Mesdames." Addie was not saving postage but showing her contempt for both convention and the women by making them share the same humiliation. In *The Honey Pot*, Cecil Fox, a bogus plutocrat, sends three separate letters to three different women, all ex-mistresses, informing each of them that he is dying and about to name an heir. Finally, both films illustrate Mankiewicz's penchant for working literature and music into the plot; Shakespeare and Brahms in *Wives*; Ben Jonson, Ponchielli, and Puccini in *The Honey Pot*. But there end the similarities. *Wives* is a movie in the true sense; it belongs on the screen. *The Honey Pot* is literature; it belongs in a library.

A Letter to Three Wives (1949)

Wives was Mankiewicz's first popular success for reasons that are not hard to fathom. Comedy of characterization was his forte, and the flashback with voice-over narration was a technique at which he excelled but which he had not used in a script since *The Keys of the Kingdom*. *Wives* had to be a flashback film. Once the letter arrives, as it does early in the plot, the action must go back in time before it can move ahead.

To appreciate what Mankiewicz achieved, one should examine the film's source: a *Cosmopolitan* short story (August 1945), "One of Our

Rex Harrison as Cecil Fox, the Volpone figure in The Honey Pot. *(Credit: Margaret Herrick Library)*

Hearts," that the author, John Klempner, expanded into a novel, *Letter to Five Wives* (1946). Mankiewicz is not even certain that he read the novel. He did not have to; he could work from Vera Caspary's treatment. Klempner's novel lacked the two main qualities of a Mankiewicz film: wit and humanity. Klempner's idea of wit can be seen in his description of Addie as a woman unable to control "some inner urge caused by the rustle of a pair of pants." And in stereotypes, there is no humanity.

Everything about the novel betrayed its magazine fiction origins, including pegging the plot on the monthly meeting of a women's club that had brought the three wives together when Addie's letter arrived. Mankiewicz abandoned the coffee klatch for a picnic excursion— something to which the average moviegoer could at least relate.

When one considers the lengths to which Mankiewicz goes to universalize his material, it is surprising that he is so often accused of being literary; except for *The Honey Pot*, he has rarely been literary. Mankiewicz is *literate*; that is, he takes what is literary—multiple point of view, for example—and gives it a rhythm and style that make it cinematic, so that the result is no less literate but no longer literary. There has been a transference, not a transcendence or a diminution, for multiple point of view can be just as complex in a film as it is in a novel.

It is the same with the flashback; as a literary device, the flashback is as old as Homer's *Odyssey*, if not older. But the Mankiewicz flashback is not a verbal conduit to the past or a transitional crutch like "It seems only yesterday that. . . ." His flashbacks are completely cinematic; with Mankiewicz, the proper integration of the flashback with the narrative flow is as much a matter of rhythm as plotting. A filmmaker must be able to determine how much of the past can be dramatized at any given time; at what point the action should return to the present; what bridging techniques to use; whether similarly shaped objects might be dissolved into each other to effect a smoother transition, etc.

Wives is a model screenplay, something quite different from a model play. But it might not have been so exemplary if it had not been for Zanuck. In her treatment, Caspary reduced the five wives of the novel to four; Mankiewicz's original script, dated 28 April 1948 and completed about five weeks before filming was scheduled to begin, was still entitled *A Letter to Four Wives* and featured four couples: Brad and Deborah Bishop, the handsome executive and his unfashionable wife; George and Rita Phipps, a high school English teacher and his radio writer-wife; Porter Hollingsway, the owner of a department store chain, and Lora May, who married him to cross over to the other side of the tracks; Roger and Martha Stewart, a struggling lawyer and the wife for whom he would like to do more but is financially unable.

Zanuck argued that the removal of the Stewarts would result in a better film; and Mankiewicz, never one for waste, salvaged what he could of the Stewart subplot. Originally, Stewart had given his wife an Easter hat that Addie selected; now Brad has Deborah buy a dress he saw Addie wear at a concert. Stewart's passion for fishing goes to George Phipps, and the gifts that Addie bought for the Stewarts' son become a birthday present for George.

Zanuck was correct; a three-part flashback with prologue is about all a 100-minute movie can accommodate. The prologue sets the film's tone; it is spoken by a woman who identifies herself but who never appears. Her voice is droll and teasing, inviting us not to take it seriously but implying that if we do not, we will pay for it: "To begin with, all the incidents and characters in this story might be fictitious, and any resemblance to you—or me—might be purely coincidental."

The prologue is a good example of what Kracauer would call contrapuntal asynchronism; that is, voice-over and visuals that are at odds with each other. The woman's voice is so mockingly fey and provocative, and the scenes of station wagon suburbia are so dull and ordinary, that one can readily understand why Addie Ross would be the main source of excitement.

Like an experienced hostess, the voice provides the introductions, taking us first to the Bishops. It is one of those disembodied voices that does not respect privacy and cuts into conversations whenever it chooses. After Deborah (Jeanne Crain) leaves to pick up Rita (Ann Sothern), the women drive along, wondering why they always end up talking about Addie Ross. "Maybe it's because if you girls didn't talk about me, you just wouldn't talk at all," the voice answers. Now one knows to whom the voice belongs.

Mankiewicz works gradually. As yet, we do not know where Deborah and Rita are headed; when they reach the pier, the third wife appears, Lora May (Linda Darnell). Now we discover they are chaperones for a picnic excursion sponsored by the local settlement house. And it is just before the boat leaves that Addie's letter arrives.   Since each wife would be given a flashback, Mankiewicz had to decide in what order the flashbacks would occur; he settled on the order of appearance: Deborah, Rita, and Lora May. His reasoning had as much to do with rhetoric as with symmetry. Mankiewicz was using the classical figure of *gradatio* or progression in terms of increasing importance. Thus he started with the least interesting couple, the Bishops. However, Brad Bishop is vital to the dénouement since he is the one husband unaccounted for at the end of the film. Beginning and ending with the Bishops allows for an effective contrast, with the least significant couple acquiring a nominal importance.

Once Mankiewicz decided upon the order of the flashbacks, he could determine their mode of visualization. There is nothing more unimaginative than the flashback that simply occurs when a character, looking wrapt withal, dematerializes into a lap dissolve and emerges in another time frame. More creative is the flashback occasioned by a memory; and more cinematic is the catalytic image or sound that sparks the memory.

The first flashback is a combination of voice-over, natural sound (noise, to be exact), and dissolve. A fairy tale that one of her charges is reading prompts Deborah to apply the opening sentence to herself: "Once upon a time there was a poor girl who was very beautiful." Then Addie's voice invades her thoughts, reminding her when another poor but beautiful girl, a farmer's daughter and ex-Wave, was introduced to suburban society at the country club dance: "Do you remember your first night in town? That was a first Saturday in May, too. Is it Brad? Is it Brad?" The chug chug of the diesels adds a persistent rhythm to Addie's question as the fairy-tale princess, the farm girl who won Prince Charming, is transported back to that disastrous May evening. The first flashback ends as it began: with a close-up of Deborah's face as Addie's voice repeats in rhythm with the diesels, "Is it Brad?"

Rita, the second to be introduced, has the second flashback. She lights a cigarette, and as the smoke is wafted upward, Addie's voice starts planting seeds of doubt: "Why didn't George go fishing? Why the blue suit?" The scene dissolves to a shot of a small clock radio in the Phipps home—an appropriate object to fade in on since Rita is a writer of radio soaps.

Mankiewicz connects the flashbacks by repeating images and motifs that emphasize the fact that it is the same ordeal the women are facing, even though the three of them are temperamentally and socially different. It is not easy to express unity in diversity or evoke similarities amid differences, but Mankiewicz succeeds. Deborah's flashback comes to an end as she spots her husband on the veranda with the always unseen Addie, a plume of cigarette smoke denoting her presence. The second flashback begins with Rita's lighting a cigarette. In each flashback, Addie's presence is felt in some way: in the first, as a trail of cigarette smoke; in the second, as a record sent to George as a birthday present; in the last, as a picture in a silver frame.

The first two flashbacks opened with the wives involved in an act of preparation: Deborah's getting dressed for the dinner dance and Rita's completing the arrangements for the dinner party she is giving for her radio producers, the Manleighs. The second flashback is longer and better developed because the Phippses are more interesting than the Bishops. Yet it is not the flashback most audiences remember; the favorite has always been the last because, of the three couples, Porter (Paul Douglas) and Lora May are the most representative—trading wisecracks and going through the tifts, estrangements, and reconciliations that are typical of married life.

Still, the second is the best written; it could easily be excerpted as a vignette. To appreciate what Mankiewicz has accomplished, one would have to read the novel in which the George character, called Josh, is a plant manager; and Rita, a short story writer. Possibly because he came from a family where teaching was so highly regarded, Mankiewicz made George an English teacher, coerced into hosting a dinner that was beyond his means and given for a couple representing everything his profession was intended to correct. Having chosen parallelism as the mode of plot development, Mankiewicz turned the dinner party into a two-part set of variations on the themes of education and ignorance, pop culture and the arts.

Mankiewicz was not setting up a dialectic since he had no intention of resolving such opposites; he wanted them to remain as bipolar as possible. Yet he could not sacrifice drama for debate, not was he willing to settle for an easy topic of satire: the folly of ignorance. Instead, he allowed the action to proceed from a clash between the Manleighs, who regard radio drama as "the literature of today," and George, who regards literature as something like Shakespeare's *Twelfth Night*.

George cannot be an intellectual snob, and Kirk Douglas's wonderfully sincere performance prevents his becoming one. Initially, he is not out to expose the Manleighs, whose ignorance flows freely because it is unimpeded by knowledge. When Mr. Manleigh, proud of his small (but inaccurate) Latin, remarks, "Tempo fugit. Right, Professor?" George smiles and answers, "Almost," instead of reminding him that it is *tempus fugit*. Nor does George guffaw when Mrs. Manleigh comes out with a double entendre. Extolling radio for its penetrative power, she notes that Sadie, the Phipps maid (played by the unforgettable Thelma Ritter), may not know it, but everytime she turns on the radio, she is being penetrated. George's wry rejoinder, "It's a good thing she didn't hear you say that," washes over Mrs. Manleigh, who is impenetrable herself.

George only assumes the role of teacher when Mrs. Manleigh, in her haste to turn on the radio, accidentally breaks a phonograph record which happens to be of the Brahms B-flat Piano Concerto; then George starts correcting his guests' grammar and lecturing them on the mediocrity of radio. Although it may seem that Mankiewicz is elevating George at the expense of his inferiors, he is really staging an *agon* between the narrow-minded and the liberally educated by showing how the Manleighs' mentality produces a culture where oozy organ music is deemed superior to Brahms; and where *The Confessions of Brenda Brown* is considered worthier than *Twelfth Night*. These were not examples Mankiewiez picked at random; rather, they were carefully chosen to fit the plot. The Brahms was a birthday gift from Addie; on the card accompanying it, she had written, "If music be the food of love, play on"—the opening line of *Twelfth Night,* the play they had done in high school together and the one that George's school is planning to present.

Since there was no reference to *Twelfth Night* in the novel, Mankiewicz could have picked any play, but none would have yielded a description that characterized George so accurately—as a man thoroughly committed to the arts and eager to share that commitment with a woman. Also, few other plays could have provided such a good parallel to the film's plot. It would not be flattering Addie's intelligence to suggest that her association with *Twelfth Night* not only inspired the inscription but also the letter. In the play, Maria, Sir Toby Belch, and Sir Andrew Aguecheek deceive Malvolio by forging a letter from Olivia, declaring that she is in love with Malvolio and encouraging him to reciprocate by performing actions that, in effect, Olivia loathes.

Art is never accidental, nor was Mankiewicz's choice of Brahms, a composer who never knew the love of a woman; and of *Twelfth Night,* a comedy in which a letter reveals the true self and characters fall in love with the illusion before they know the reality.

The second flashback ends as the first did—with a fiasco. As George says, "I want my wife back," the camera moves in for a medium close-up of Rita. Addie's voice asks again, "Why didn't George go fishing? And

Ann Sothern and Linda Darnell as two of the title characters in
A Letter to Three Wives. *(Credit: Movie Star News)*

why the blue suit?" Finally, the scene dissolves to a close-up of Rita back at the picnic.

The third flashback repeats the voice-over/natural sound/dissolve pattern of the first. The picnic is in progress; in the bathhouse locker room, Lora May boasts to Rita, "I've got everything I want." The pipe under the sink is leaking, and Addie's voice merges with the steady thud of the water dripping into a pail: "Maybe you haven't got everything you wanted after all." The leaking pipe dissolves to a leaking sink with the water also trickling into a pail. The action has shifted to the kitchen of the Finney home where Lora May lived with her mother and sister before she married Porter Hollingsway.

The third flashback emphasizes characterization. Dramatically, little happens except that Lora May Finney succeeds in becoming Mrs. Porter Hollingsway. Since Mankiewicz's Lora May was not the "little, bustling, efficient" Southern belle she was in the novel, he had to keep her from falling into the ways of a gold digger. Living so close to the wrong side of the tracks that everything in the kitchen rattles when the train passes by has made her upwardly, but not brazenly, mobile. Linda Darnell found the key to Lora May in a cynicism that had not hardened into contempt, and an aggressiveness that had not soured into egomania. Paul Douglas made Porter oafishly sincere—a tycoon who wanted a woman of class to share his over-furnished mansion, not realizing that he had such a woman in Lora May. What both of them have in common is that they have advanced from the vulgar to the ostentatious. But what makes them endearing is the fact that ambition has not sapped their humanity. Porter is a huggable nouveau riche (a "big gorilla," as Lora May affectionately calls him at the end); and she is a man-trapper who fell in love with her prey.

Always conscious of the integration that comes from repeating motifs, Mankiewicz ends the last flashback where he began it—in the Finney kitchen as a passing train sends out vibrations, this time to Lora May and Porter who are literally getting off to a shaky start. Having used a form dissolve to move the action from the picnic grounds to the kitchen, Mankiewicz could not use another to return to the present. Since the outing and the flashbacks have come to an end, he fades out on the reverberating kitchen and in on the docking boat, with a dissolve to the pier where everyone disembarks.

A Letter to Three Wives exemplifies one of the most imaginative uses of the flashback in American film: three graduated flashbacks linked thematically, visually, and aurally and reflecting various types of comedy—farce in the first where Deborah's gown comes apart on the dance floor; high comedy in the second; and low comedy in the third.

Ultimately, Mankiewicz must reveal the identity of the errant husband. One might have expected him to have the wives return home in the same order as they left, thereby making the last wife the one who lost her husband to Addie. But this would be too obvious; of the three husbands, Porter would be the most likely to succumb to Addie's charms since he regards her as the epitome of class. Mankiewicz chose a different order of return—Rita, Deborah, Lora May—because the narrative emphasis has shifted from the wives to the husbands, one of whom is at home; one of whom is not; and one of whom is late.

In the novel, Rita's was the husband who strayed; but since there is no similarity between Josh and George, one can hardly expect George to do the same. He may be a liberal but not a libertine. Thus, it would make sense to eliminate George immediately and have Rita find him at home. Why didn't he go fishing? Why the blue suit? His high school called, asking him to direct *Twelfth Night*, a play for which his experience with the Manleighs has made him eminently qualified.

Two possibilities remain: Brad and Porter. It is definitely Porter, one feels. Yet Mankiewicz seems to discourage that possibility by having Deborah learn from the butler that a woman phoned with a message: "Mr. Bishop called to say he is very sorry; he will not be home tonight." As Deborah reads the message to herself, Addie's voice reads it to us. It would then seem to be Brad; the first husband to appear is the husband who will not be seen again. And one would be partially right; Brad will not reappear.

Even those who have seen *Wives* more than once have difficulty remembering which husband ran off with Addie. The reason is that the narrative logic leads to a conclusion that is contradicted by the denouement. There is a similar conflict between the logical and the actual resolution of *The Blue Dahlia* (1946). Raymond Chandler originally intended the murderer to be a World War II veteran suffering from constant headaches because of a steel plate in his head. But Washington intervened, ruling that a movie with a murderous vet would be bad for morale. Chandler had to make the killer the house detective, although the evidence suggests otherwise. Even the buffs keep forgetting the killer's identity because the visuals point to one character and the script to another.

Although Porter tells Lora May he is the guilty husband, one is not entirely convinced. Certainly it was one of the shortest disappearances in the history of adultery, lasting about as long as the picnic. There is no doubt that Porter's confession alleviates Deborah's anxiety and makes him a hero to Lora May; and the film seems to end with Addie's defeat—or does it? In the final shot, Deborah's unused cocktail glass mysteriously topples over and cracks as Addie's voice sighs: "Heigh-ho. Goodnight, everybody." Does the breaking of the glass signal the end of Addie's power or the opposite; namely, that something of her ability to shatter harmony still remains?

There are more unanswered questions. Who was the woman who phoned the Bishops' residence? If it were Brad's secretary, she would have identified herself. Did Mankiewicz use Addie's voice to read the message because she was the woman or because Deborah assumed she was? Did *any* of the husbands spend the day with Addie, or was the letter a hoax like the one in *Twelfth Night*, designed to give three women the most unsettling day of their lives? Did Porter confess because he assumed Brad was the truant husband and tried to cover up for him out of compassion for Deborah?

It hardly seems likely that most moviegoers would question the resolution. Yet if asked a month later to name the husband, how many could? Mankiewicz, who had a disastrous experience with Lubitsch while shooting *Dragonwyck,* succeeded in making a film with the Lubitsch touch, a "Did they or didn't they?" movie in which we believe what we do not see and see what we do not believe. No matter what Lubitsch thought of Mankiewicz, he certainly would have appreciated the tantalizing ambiguity of the denouement.

The Honey Pot (1967)

Wives is not the kind of film that can be remade, nor is the plot device one that can withstand repeated use. For every *Wives* there are ten movies like *A Letter for Evie* (1945). But the letter motif still haunted Mankiewicz; one can therefore understand his attraction to Thomas Sterling's novel, *The Evil of the Day* (1955), which Frederick Knott dramatized as *Mr. Fox of Venice. The Evil of the Day* was rather stylish for an Inner Sanctum mystery. Suggested by Ben Jonson's *Volpone,* it was the kind of novel that flattered those who knew the source and could appreciate how Jonson's Volpone ("Fox") and Mosca ("Fly") became Cecil Fox and his secretary, William Fieramosca ("Proudfly"); and how Jonson's Celia and Voltore became Celia Johns and Henry Voltor.

The conceit appealed to Mankiewicz; so did the premise: reality overstepping the boundaries of illusion, encroaching on a too perfect world and finally rendering it ordinary. Cecil Fox inhabits a Venetian palazzo that itself is a microcosm of the novel in which the plot details of an Elizabethan play are intertwined with the conventions of contemporary detective fiction. Similarly, in the palazzo, illusion confronts reality; an actual staircase faces one sketched on a wall, and real chairs stand next to painted ones. The interweaving of the real and the illusory also characterizes the charade that Fox has arranged for three old acquaintances whom he invites to Venice on the pretext that he is dying and as yet has no heir. The charade belongs to the world of make believe; it is Fox's version of *Volpone* with himself in the lead and his secretary as stage manager. But the audience is real, and the ruse is misanthropic

enough to be plausible. Fox loves the unnatural; hence his affinity for
Venice with its man-made canals which he considers a triumph over
natural waterways. One expects the deception to have a silken perver-
sity, an amoral gratuitousness since there is nothing Fox can gain from
two of his guests, except the pleasure of watching them fawn over him.
Anson Simms, a religious enthusiast, has dissipated his fortune; Henry
Voltor, a solicitor, is living off his family's name. But the charade is not
diabolical enough; the twist it needs can only come about if events take a
bizarre turn: if the third guest, Mrs. Sheridan, Fox's former common-
law wife and the only one of the trio with any money, arrives, expecting
to be made Fox's heir, and by her death makes him hers.

Since *The Evil of the Day* was an Inner Sanctum mystery, one
expected a murder, a police inspector, and an investigation; Sterling
delivered on all counts. But since the author created the equivalent of a
romantic duo in Fieramosca and Celia, he must pair them off, and does.
In *The Honey Pot*, Mankiewicz's adaptation, all these motifs are present
along with others from the novel—the timepieces the would-be heirs
bring Fox, the crucial roll of quarters, the dumbwaiter that makes Fox's
room accessible to Celia. However, Mankiewicz's principal change was
in the trio who became three women: Merle McGill (Edie Adams),
Princess Dominique (Capucine), and Lone Star (Susan Hayward), the
Mrs. Sheridan figure, whose secretary is called Nurse Sarah Watkins
(Maggie Smith) instead of Celia.

Mankiewicz now had the rudiments of a companion piece to *A Letter
to Three Wives*. However, he used *Volpone* quite differently than he
used *Twelfth Night* in the earlier film. *Volpone* is to *The Honey Pot* what
the originals were to Picasso's *Paraphrases of Old Masters:* a point of
departure. Fox's feigning death to trick three people into coming to
Venice parallels Volpone's deathbed deception to extract what he could
from his greedy friends. Volpone willingly took gifts even from those
who could not afford to give them; Fox accepts the trio's presents as if
they were tribute, knowing that two of the women are in financial
difficulty. Mankiewicz also made more of *Volpone* than Sterling did; *The
Honey Pot* opens with Fox attending a private performance of the play
which he terminates abruptly in the fifth act at a point that later becomes
an important clue.

If the situation sounds vaguely Pirandellian, it is because the characters are also actors in their own scenarios. Fox based his charade on the
deathbed trick in *Volpone* and hired an out-of-work actor, McFly (Cliff
Robertson), as stage manager. Since Fox's scenario has no denouement,
Mankiewicz allows two of the characters, Dominique and Sarah, to
provide a joint one, thereby making them coauthors as well as persons of
the drama. According to the rules of the game—the same rules that
govern the self-begetting novel in which the protagonist is conscious of

himself as an author—one judges such characters not in terms of lifelikeness and plausibility but rather in terms of their ability to create lifelikeness and plausibility, just as one judges sleuths like Hercule Poirot and Miss Marple on their skill at solving cases, not on the credibility of those cases.

The Honey Pot is a case to be solved; at midpoint, it becomes a whodunit. But much earlier, at the beginning, in fact, Mankiewicz makes it clear that it is a film with clues. Fox stops the performance of *Volpone* in act 5, scene 2, with "Hold, here's my will," thus giving Mankiewicz another link between *The Honey Pot* and *Wives*: the heir whose identity will be withheld until the end like the errant husband's in the other film. In Jonson, Mosca became Volpone's heir, but it would be too easy—and obvious—for McFly to become Fox's. Besides, *The Honey Pot* is not *Volpone* neat; it is, as Plato might say, four degrees removed from the original: Jonson as revamped by Sterling as dramatized by Knott as adapted by Mankiewicz.

In the course of its evolution into a film, the plot changed from a comic satire to a baroque whodunit where what mattered was less the turn of the screw than the gilding of the filigree. By appropriating the conventions of the whodunit and embellishing them to hide their lowly origins, Mankiewicz achieved one of his goals: the triumph of style over the banality of life. But it was a Pyrrhic victory; once *The Honey Pot* developed into a film about the conflict between life and art, form overshadowed characterization, and the interplay between the real and the ideal assumed greater importance than the players. Self-conscious art exacts a price, and in *The Honey Pot* everybody pays. Since Mankiewicz has given his characters coauthor status, they are responsible for the success or failure of their scenarios, just as he is responsible for integrating those scenarios within his film.

Except for the finale, Fox's scenario is derivative. Although Jonson's *Volpone* drew on character types and themes in Roman comedy, it was not consciously based on any particular Plautine play. But Cecil Fox is working from the *Volpone* premise, resorting to imitation of the most basic sort. Jonson made disguise integral to the plot, for example, in a scene in which Volpone masquerades as a mountebank. Fox does not traffic in disguise, only deception. It might have been better if he attempted a disguise or two, like Foxwell J. Sly, the Volpone figure in Larry Gelbart's *Sly Fox* (1976). When disguise is intrinsic to the action, it is judged in terms of the play, not the player. But Fox's play is as limited as his acting ability. He is, as McFly notes, a "sloppy performer." A cardiac invalid does not have empty liquor bottles in his room.

Since McFly realizes that life can "louse up" a script, he is more conscious of particulars than Fox, whose contempt for life, at least as it is lived by ordinary folk, makes him impatient with details. Unlike the

Elizabethans who baited bears, Fox baits humans, especially women. In one of the cruellest scenes in any film, Dominique comes to his room to seek assurance that she will be his heir; dutifully bearing her gift, she enters with an hourglass filled with gold dust. It is a loveless encounter for both of them; their eyes meeting in close-up as they play cat and mouse. Fox not only confronts her with the fact that she is penniless but also punishes her for her understandable avarice by subjecting her to a seduction attempt so impersonal that it is demeaning. As he methodically unbuttons her suit jacket, the camera stays on his fastidious fingers which are not even excited by the flash of white from her bra. The unbuttoning is more erotic for the audience than it is for Fox, who considers it a trial: "It isn't easy for a man when a woman needs him more than he needs her," he laments. McFly's timely entrance spares Dominique further humiliation.

Fox is also the closet ballet dancer he was in the novel, but even in this role his performance is lackluster. He is just a bedroom leaper, whirling about to the "Dance of the Hours." His taste in music is quite revealing. Ponchielli's "Dance of the Hours" is familiar, good-natured, and vigorous; it is also musically undistinguished. Yet its superficiality suited Fox, who lived amid art without being ennobled by it. He also lived by the books—literally; for the books in the palazzo were all that was his. Whether he read them, except for *Volpone*, is another matter. A single work is often enough to make one a story figure. The furniture was rented from movie studios, as would befit a man who wanted soundstage perfection from life.

The "Dance of the Hours" is also a ballet about time, one of the major themes in the novel and the film. In each, the trio present Fox with a timepiece. In the film, Dominique brings an hourglass; Lone Star, an antique clock; and Myrtle, a slab-encased one. Before Fox commits suicide, he smashes each of them in a transcendent gesture, relinquishing a world where life's pleasures are clocked for one that exists outside of time and therefore impervious to chronometry. As he explained earlier to Sarah, the connoisseur knows how to savor time, slowing down when life is good, accelerating when it is bad; while the little people, lacking all sense of rhythm, swallow time like hamburgers—a homely simile but one that foreshadows the manner of Fox's exit.

The only way Fox can conquer time is to do the opposite of what the little people do. If time is golden, then it should be consumed as gold, not as hamburger. If Fox could devour the gold of time, he would not only triumph over the temporal; he would also have a bravura finish to his *Volpone* charade that would make up in showmanship what it lacked in originality. As McFly observed, Fox took it with him—"it" being the gold dust which he ingested by hollowing out chocolates, filling them with the gold, adding barbiturates, and washing it all down with whiskey. The sands of time that mortals traverse have become grains of gold for Fox. In consuming the gold dust, he has foiled destiny by emptying its hourglass and transforming its contents by an alchemy of the will. Born a man, he dies a god—or so he thinks.

It was the ultimate in snobbish suicide, but ingenious enough to redeem his *Volpone*. However, it is only the penultimate act. Mankiewicz is adhering to the premise of shared authorship. Since Dominique and Sarah are also authors, Mankiewicz allows them to collaborate on the final act.

Dominique admits that the gold dust was really colored sand, thus vulgarizing what otherwise would have been a decadent demise. Dominique's revelation only begins the last act. One should recall that Fox interrupted the performance of *Volpone* at the moment the title character said, "Hold, here's my will." Lone Star's murder and Fox's suicide have relegated the will to the background. But the space for the heir has not been filled in. Since Fox's estate is mortgaged to the hilt, it would be useless to any heir. So, purely as a lark, Sarah asks McFly to write in her name. He complies, not realizing that, as Fox's heir, Sarah would inherit Lone Star's estate which is considerable. Sarah's deception concludes the last act and the film as well; because she is in love with McFly, she agrees to give him the money if he marries her and enrolls in law school.

Fox is furious about the new ending, expressing his indignation from the other world: "If just once, the bloody script turned out the way we wrote it," he sighs to Lone Star. It may be Dantean for murderer and victim to occupy the same circle; but in this case, the two seem to enjoy each other's company—which may suggest that they had to die to appreciate what they had in common.

"Let the folks go home," Lone Star begs of her testy companion. And when they did, one wonders what they made of *The Honey Pot*. Would they appreciate Fox's wish that the script turn out as written—the wish of every screenwriter? And would they understand that, subtextually, *The Honey Pot* was a film about film, using as an example a case of single authorship that mushroomed into a collaboration, culminating in the original author's being denied his choice of ending? And if moviegoers failed to perceive the various levels on which the film was working, could they be blamed?

The Honey Pot is a film of sources and analogues; graphically, it would look like a series of concentric circles. On still another level, it is a film about adaptation, a subject Mankiewicz knows well, and how the material of others is absorbed into a new setting where it is reduced to an evocation or a nuance. For example, the "Dance of the Hours" is an analogue; it comes from Ponchielli's opera, *La Gioconda* (1876), which ends with the lovers going off together and the heroine's suicide, which, roughly, is what happens at the conclusion of *The Honey Pot.*

Even Fox's monologue on time originated elsewhere—in Sterling's novel. Sterling provided the idea which Mankiewicz personalized. Sterling's "Look at this clock. . . . But do you think it gives a damn whether it measures good or bad time? No, it doesn't know anything about it" becomes Mankiewicz's "There's good time and bad time. Does a clock give a damn about what kind of time it measures? No. But we do—we special ones."

The film's denouement, which derives from neither Jonson nor Sterling, is not without literary precedent. Sarah's trick was anticipated by Gianni Schicchi, whom Dante placed in the eighth circle of hell and whom Puccini made the hero of his one-act opera of the same name. In the opera, the heirs of Buoso Donati prevail upon Gianni Schicchi to impersonate the dead Buoso and dictate a new will, giving them what they believe is theirs. Schicchi complied by willing most of Buoso's fortune to himself.

One usually speaks of sources and analogues in a literary rather than a filmic context—for example, Shakespeare's narrative and dramatic sources, Chaucer's analogues, etc. Discussing *The Honey Pot* in such terms may flatter the screenwriter but it damns the director with faint praise. The screenplay of *The Honey Pot* is one of the densest in American film, with so many levels of meaning that excavation rather than interpretation seems in order. But it is a work of literature, not of cinema. Usually, Mankiewicz has been able to distinguish between the literate and the literary, writing scripts that were never less than literate but never in competition with literature. The best Mankiewicz scripts were meant to be visualized; while they can be read and studied as models of screenwriting, their natural habitat has always been the screen.

It may be pointless to suggest what *The Honey Pot* might have been; but since Mankiewicz was working with the same plot device he used in *Wives,* he might have gone one step further and reduced Fox to a presence as he did Addie Ross. Of course, it would have meant one less film role for Rex Harrison or anybody else. But if Addie had been a character, her story would have been in competition with the others, just as Fox's *Volpone* is in competition with Mankiewicz's life versus art subtext, Dominique's twist, and Sarah's denouement. Fox also grows tiresome; he may think he belongs in the seventeenth century but he lacks that period's main characteristic—genius. All he has in common with it is his affinity for the "Dance of the Hours," which comes from an opera set in seventeenth-century Venice; an opera whose four-hour length is only justified by the heroine's great last-act aria, "Suicidio," just as Fox's own showpiece suicide redeems his rather vapid *Volpone*.

Mankiewicz also wore his learning more gracefully in *Wives*, working *Twelfth Night* into the plot so subtly that one is unaware of its being a point of reference. None of the wives says she came upon a copy of the play, as Sarah says of *Volpone*, and that it has some bearing on 'the present situation.

For all its brilliance, *The Honey Pot* is disappointing. It is as if Mankiewicz suffered a loss of self-assurance and tried to establish his credentials as an intellectual, as if we did not know he was one.

5

Family and Race

House of Strangers (1949)

ALTHOUGH PHILIP YORDAN of *Anna Lucasta* (1944) fame is billed as the screenwriter of *House of Strangers*, the script is virtually Mankiewicz's. Yordan had been hired to adapt a brief segment of Jerome Weidman's *I'll Never Go There Any More*. The results were disappointing, and Zanuck turned the project over to Mankiewicz, who discarded Yordan's dialogue and substituted his own. Since he refused to share screen credits with Yordan, his name appeared only as the film's director.[1]

Co-credit would not have made much difference since *House of Strangers* was not on a par with *The Late George Apley, The Ghost and Mrs. Muir,* and *A Letter to Three Wives.* Mankiewicz had the same problem with it that he had with *Dragonwyck*: competing plots. The one that would bring out the real Mankiewicz would have been the subplot: the love affair between Irene Bennett (Susan Hayward), a playgirl from Central Park West, and Max Monetti (Richard Conte), an East Side lawyer. Interestingly, the film's working title was *East Side Story.* However, the central figure was Max's father, Gino Monetti (Edward G. Robinson), an Italian immigrant who caught the brass ring, American style, and advanced from barber to banker, creating a family bank with three of his sons—Joseph, Tony, and Pietro—as president, first and second vice-presidents respectively of the Monetti Trust; and Max as the bank's attorney.

By its very nature, the film was bipolar: East Side/West Side, family drama/love story, ethnic dialogue/cool, sexy banter. It was also the kind of film that could degenerate into ethnic stereotypy. However, Man-

Edward G. Robinson as Gino Monetti in House of Strangers.
(Credit: Movie Star News)

77

kiewicz restrained Robinson and kept him from turning Gino into an "Eye-talian" patriarch. Generally, Robinson was effective, especially in his self-pitying vendetta monologue in which he begged Max to avenge him when his sons assumed control of the bank. However, except for Robinson, Esther Minciotti (Mrs. Monetti), Luther Adler (Joe), and Richard Conte, the rest of the Monetti clan lacked authenticity. The nadir was Hope Emerson's Helena. Emerson, who is best remembered as the sadistic prison matron of *Caged* (1950), sounded as if she were rehearsing that role with an Italian accent.

Since the Monettis never become more than a house of strangers, they remain unknowable. Mankiewicz may have felt the same way, since he reserved his best dialogue for Max and Irene, generating more sexual electricity between them than ever passed between Lora May and Porter. In fact, the Max-Irene subplot held such interest for Mankiewicz that he rushed into it without supplying suitable background information. Usually, Mankiewicz anticipates questions a moviegoer might have about a character; yet who Irene is, how she can live in such luxury, how she heard about Max in the first place are unclear. She is a younger version of Vera in Rodgers and Hart's *Pal Joey* (1940)—bewitched, bothered, but more bewildering than bewildered.

Nonetheless, Hayward gave Irene the glamour of a butterfly in a diamond chrysalis, a sensuousness cut to the perfection of a baguette. In every way, she is Max's superior. When she wants to leave for dinner, Max delivers a "Me Tarzan, you Jane" lecture. Finally, when *he* decides that he is ready, he walks to the door. Irene stays exactly where she is, slowly removing her ermine wrap and tossing it on a chair. Mankiewicz frames the shot with Max in the doorway and Irene standing defiantly in the background. Lubitsch might have closed the door, but Mankiewicz thought it would be sexier to leave it open, with the lovers momentarily frozen in their positions; he was right.

Max has only one chance to show some muscle: when he slaps Irene in the face. Mankiewicz wanted Max to strike her twice, but Zanuck intervened; once was enough. Clearly it is Irene who has the upper hand. Like Lora May, she will not tolerate an unresponsive lover. On the dance floor, she realizes that Max's thoughts are elsewhere. When they return to their table, she announces that she is leaving. "I'm hungry," Max growls. "So eat," she replies, sweeping past him as the waiter is about to serve the soup.

It would seem, then, that Mankiewicz has made two films: one about Irene and Max, the other about the Monettis. It is true that the plots do not mesh harmoniously; yet Mankiewicz tried to have them complement each other by stressing elements common to both. In each plot the characters suffer from a perception of themselves and others that has little or no foundation in reality. Irene expects strict fidelity from Max, who wants docility from her. At one point, Irene, who is always walking out on Max when he fails to live up to her expectations, leaves him abruptly during a boxing match; he catches up with her at the exit. For a moment, they resolve their differences and embrace, right of frame, while the fight continues behind them. This juxtaposition of romance and reality was Mankiewicz's way of expressing the tension between the ideal and the real. The embrace is striking by its frontality, and so in accord with what one expects from love, Hollywood style, that one almost forgets that two men are slugging it out in the background. Later, when Irene contemplates leaving Max for someone else, the two rivals face each other, with Irene's face reflected in the wall mirror between them—the ideal in the midst of the real.

A similar tension exists in the Monetti plot in which Mankiewicz also balances opposites: the man and the mask, the actuality and the dream. From Gino Monetti's benign portrait that dominates the living room, one might think he was a benefactor, a humanitarian; and at times his actions do reflect a generous spirit. But more often, the man is not his portrait; he is a usurer who garnishees wages.

Although there are no references in the script to the portrait, it is a visual presence as vital to the plot as any line of dialogue. The portrait is the ideal against which the reality is contrasted and measured. When Irene denounces Gino, he stands in front of his portrait—the mask overlooking the man. At Gino's wake, the portrait stares down at the closed coffin.

For a Mankiewicz film, *House of Strangers* has considerable visual power. Even the opening and closing scenes complement each other visually, fitting together like halves of a circle as illusion and reality are brought into a state of temporary closure. The means is the staircase of the Monetti home. The film is a flashback, beginning with Max's return after a seven-year prison term. Max stands by the mantel, looking up at the portrait. He puts on a recording of his father's favorite aria, "M'appari," from von Flotow's *Martha* (1847). As Max listens to the sweet but plangent music, the camera, in an unbroken shot, tracks out of the living room, up the staircase and past the first landing to the very top of the steps, stopping at the second landing window which, through a virtually unnoticeable dissolve, turns into the same window seven years earlier. As the curtains billow in the breeze, the camera tracks across to the bedroom, inching its way into the bathroom where Gino is scrubbing himself vigorously, bellowing "M'appari"—the real drowning out the ideal.

The flashback ended as it began—with the record. Now it is stuck, as if the idealized world it represented had become mired in reality. "M'appari" has been silenced, but the staircase has one more function to perform. It symbolized the ascent to power for Gino; it will represent the consolidation of power for his son Joe. It was Joe who had been responsible for Max's imprisonment. When Joe had learned that his brother was planning to bribe a juror to save Gino from being indicted for misappropriation of funds, he had informed the police. Max went to jail while the bank reverted to the control of his brothers. At the wake, Max, standing in front of the portrait, gives his brothers the sign of the vendetta: the thumb jerked violently from the mouth. Naturally, they do not want him back.

At the end, the film takes its most realistic turn. It is not the realism of location shots of Little Italy with the sepia look of old photographs that we have seen earlier; but the realism of one of the ugliest forms of family hatred—attempted fratricide. After Joe and Pietro pummel Max, they drag him up the stairs. This is not the camera ascending to the past, for it is an ascent of a different kind. The symbolism has changed to a ruthless literalism as the staircase now becomes Joe's means of reaching the terrace from which he plans to have Pietro hurl Max.

When Pietro hesitates, Joe shouts, "Dumbhead!" Pietro drops Max and lunges after Joe. But Max saves Joe from the fate intended for himself by reminding Pietro that fratricide is exactly what their father would have wanted; by murdering Joe, Pietro would be avenging the father he hated.

Just when one thinks the film will end on an appropriately somber note, the dawn comes up; and Irene and Max drive off into the sunrise. They are on the backlot of Twentieth Century-Fox, but it looks like a New York street. The sun also looks real, but the resolution is pure Hollywood. The improbable union of a tough guy lawyer and a lady of leisure needs all the sunshine it can get.

As a film, *House of Strangers* is an anomaly. At times, it seemed to be heading toward social realism but only in the form of touches and motifs: Italian restaurants with checked tablecloths and candles in wax-encrusted wine bottles; family squabbles at a dinner table dominated by a platter of spaghetti; location shots of Mulberry Street; a hint of the Great Depression; and contrasting attitudes toward poverty and affluence, the East Side and the West Side, the humble past and the ostentatious present. There is realism in *House of Strangers* but of a special kind—what is, as opposed to what seems.

Actually, *House of Strangers* is closer to *film noir.* Like the other studios. Fox went through a *noir* phase in the mid and late 1940s, although it was too serious minded to produce classic *noir*—the kind at which RKO and Universal excelled—where death-white faces peered out of the darkness; the streets glistened as if they had been paved with oil; the moon looked neon; and the sun never shone. *Film noir* almost had its own smell—acrid and heady, like perfumed sweat. However, at Fox, the photography was too sharp; the *mise-en-scène* too elaborate to generate the kind of primitive excitement of *Detour* or *Phantom Lady* (1944). Fox's *Kiss of Death* (1947) had noirish elements, as did *Cry of the City* (1948). *Laura* (1944) is sometimes designated as *film noir*. Although it seems too baroque for *noir,* it has that cankered rose look peculiar to the genre. But so does *House of Strangers*. The Monetti house reflects that intermediate stage between decadence and decay; where everything has the appearance of overly varnished wood about to warp.

The final staircase scene represents the best of *noir*: stylized evil in black and white—the white appearing enameled and congealed; the black lacquered and dried. The staircase has always been one of the key props of *noir*—for example, *The Spiral Staircase* (1946), *The Strange Love of Martha Ivers* (1948), *The Killers* (1946), etc. Mankiewicz made it more than a prop; he made it the personification of evil.

No Way Out (1950)

Although Mankiewicz has often characterized himself as apolitical, he was a liberal, at least at the time when it counted—from the 1930s to the early 1950s. He wrote the dialogue for the depression classic, *Our Daily Bread* (1934), which idealized cooperatives—as distinct from cooperative farming, Soviet-style—although some failed to see the difference. *Fury* was a strong indictment of right-wing fanaticism; *People Will Talk* (1951) satirized, perhaps too subtly, the right's mania for investigating iconoclastic intellectuals.

It would have been difficult for anyone as sensitive as Mankiewicz to be at Fox in the late 1940s without being affected by the liberal climate that Zanuck fostered with the help of screenwriters like Philip Dunne and directors like Elia Kazan and Henry Hathaway. Although Zanuck had dealt with racism in *Pinky* (1949), the film lacked any sense of urgency because the title character could pass for white. *Pinky* never went to the roots of racial hatred that fork out in so many directions that one could dig forever without locating them. Mankiewicz was at least willing to try, and *No Way Out* was the result.

When Zanuck read the script of *No Way Out*, he sent Mankiewicz a memo from Antibes (8 August 1949), calling it "the perfect combination of suspense, drama, and humanity" and noting that "it has something to say and it says it with great effectiveness." However, he refused to spend any more money on it than he did on *Pinky*, warning Mankiewicz not to go overboard on the sets. *No Way Out* hardly needed a lavish production. There was another side to Fox besides the monochromatic opulence of *Laura* and the epic technicolor of *Wilson* (1944); there was the Fox of the gritty semidocumentary (*The House on 92nd St.*, 1945; *Call Northside 777*, 1948) and crime movies like *Kiss of Death*, which introduced Richard Widmark as a grinning punk who pushed a woman in a wheelchair to her death down a flight of stairs. In *No Way Out*, Mankiewicz cast Widmark as Ray Biddle, a hater of blacks, who, together with his brothers, form a trio of grotesques straight out of Flannery O'Connor or Carson McCullers, except that the setting suggests upstate New York or perhaps the Midwest—Joyce Carol Oates country. Johnny Biddle is dying of a brain tumor; George Biddle is a deaf mute; Ray is a hood with a wound in his thigh that looks as if it is suppurating rather than bleeding. But that is what racism is: life blood turned to pus.

No Way Out adopted the look and language of its subject. Although no four-letter words were used—nor could they have been at the time—the atmosphere reeked of obscenity as Biddle shouts every conceivable racial insult at Luther Brooks (Sidney Poitier), the black doctor who is treating him. When he is not calling Luther a "coon" or a "boogie," or referring to the hospital as the Cotton Club, he is blowing cigarette smoke in the doctor's face.

Since Biddle's is not a typical case of racial hatred, Mankiewicz does not reduce it to a syndrome. Biddle needs the kind of love that society cannot give any one individual. When he sees the slightest concern shown toward a minority, especially toward blacks, he reverts to childish envy, railing against pulpit appeals to "love the nigger children" because he wants that love for himself and only receives it from his brothers. When Johnny Biddle dies after Luther, suspecting a brain tumor, orders a spinal tap, Ray writhes in agony that is more emotional than physical. To him, the supreme insult was Johnny's not being treated by a white doctor. Consequently, he refuses an autopsy. Only Johnny's ex-wife, Edie (Linda Darnell), can authorize one.

Darnell was the right choice for Edie, a low grade Lora May that Porter would not even go slumming with. Mankiewicz distills every ounce of sleaze and tawdriness he can out of the scene when Dr. Wharton (Stephen McNally) and Luther call on Edie at her tenement. The first shot of Edie has her back to the camera. Even as she walks to the door, she is seen from the rear. Only when she opens the door, does one see her face. The hair is raven-black, lacquered into a sick sheen; a wave plastered down the left side of her face in imitation of Veronica Lake's peek-a-boo bang but not as free flowing. It is too impeded by oil, dirt, and spray to cascade; instead, it congeals. For the entire scene, "In a Sentimental Mood" is heard on the radio, the Big Band sound mocking the seriousness of the discussion. After the doctors leave, Edie lights a cigarette as a high shot captures her claustrophobic existence.

On the other hand, the Brooks home is spacious and uncluttered. This is the only time the film verges on the obvious, although one can understand why Mankiewicz wanted a contrast between two ways of life. Instead of "In a Sentimental Mood," Brahms's Lullaby is played on a screechy violin. The conversation centers about food and whipped cream for the apple pie; and Cora Brooks's quietly dignified "We're tired but we're here" speech is a moving moment, but one feels it belongs elsewhere.

Apart from its intrinsic ugliness, racism breeds fear of confrontation and violence. There is a race riot in the film that is never shown; instead, Mankiewicz dramatizes the preparations for it which are even more frightening. As Edie and George Biddle walk through the streets of Beaver Canal, they seem to be making a descent into hell. The whites have assembled in the junkyard, swinging metal bars at the wrecks as if to gain strength for the coming battle. "Beat a nigger," one of them calls to Edie. The camera cranes up for a high shot, culminating in a black man's crawling along a rooftop overlooking the automobile graveyard. An orchestration develops from the beating of metal on metal; the cacophony anticipating the eerie tympany that accompanies Sebastian's dismemberment in *Suddenly, Last Summer.* One of the blacks sends up a flare, turning everything spectral white. Everyone stands frozen, and

A race war about to erupt in No Way Out. *(Credit: Margaret Herrick Library)*

the battle begins in long shot. One sees the armies clash but not the actual battle; only the prelude and the aftermath as bodies are brought into the hospital.

The sequence is a masterful evocation of unseen violence. The cutting continuity indicates something about Mankiewicz that is rarely acknowledged: his ability to build a sequence from images that are variegated and arranged climactically. It is true editing-in-camera: long shot of Beaver Canal group, as a black crawls along rooftop; close shot of black with flare gun; long shot of a black, Lefty, motioning to others; medium shot of blacks with weapons entering single file; long shot of blacks outside Boot Hill; long shot of men inside junkyard as flare goes up from rooftop and blacks rush in; long shot of blacks and whites confronting each other with dissolve to County Hospital.

Although burning up with fever, Biddle insists on waging his own war—with Luther. Tricking him into coming to Wharton's house, he proceeds to degrade Luther by making him stand in the center of the room with his hands in his pockets. When Edie flicks off the lights, Luther manages to get Biddle's pistol. In the powerful final scene, Luther bends over his patient writhing in agony that is intensified by the ministrations of a black doctor. "Don't cry, white boy; you're going to live," Luther says soberly, without the bitterness one would expect. The camera tracks back dramatically, leaving Luther and Biddle at the foot of the stairs in a modified Pietà; and Edie at the door, waiting for the police whose piercing sirens herald their arrival.

No Way Out was the kind of movie that invited overkill. During his early career, Mankiewicz had a tendency toward excess that Zanuck was generally able to curb. This film made its point without the conclusion that Mankiewicz intended. *No Way Out* was to have ended in Wharton's cellar where Biddle, after killing Edie, forced Luther to hollow out a hole in the coal bin. Apart from the obvious symbolism that was not rendered any subtler by Biddle's calling his victim "Sambo," the proposed ending would have reduced the film to a study of moral rot, leaving the viewer feeling unclean instead of purged; and, worse, vindictive instead of forgiving.

Zanuck was also troubled by the script's detour into anti-Semitism during the race riot that had whites breaking the windows of a Jewish delicatessen. Having made a movie about anti-Semitism (*Gentleman's Agreement*, 1947) and one about racism (*Pinky*), Zanuck did not want any overlapping. He also wanted a conclusion with greater cathartic effect than one ending in a coal bin.

By accepting Zanuck's changes, Mankiewicz made one of the most powerful indictments of inhumanity ever filmed. Perhaps because it made so few concessions to its audience, *No Way Out* is rarely revived or telecast. Generally, when a *No Way Out* is listed for the Late Show, it is the 1972 Italian-made, English-dubbed Mafia movie with Alain Delon and Richard Conte. *Sic transit gloria,* as Mankiewicz would be the first to admit.

6

Commitment and Confusion

FOR SOMEONE WHO claimed to be "the least politically minded person in the world," Mankiewicz found himself at the center of a political controversy in 1950 that was symptomatic of the times: a loyalty oath that Cecil B. DeMille, a rabid anti-Communist, managed to make mandatory for members of the Screen Directors Guild (SDG), of which Mankiewicz was president at the time. Taking advantage of Mankiewicz's being in Europe, DeMille succeeded in getting a bylaw passed making the oath compulsory. When Mankiewicz returned, he publicly questioned the bylaw's legality in light of the Taft-Hartley Act that required the oath only of union officers such as himself. As SDG president, he had no qualms about signing the oath but objected to its being imposed upon the membership. In retaliation, DeMille attempted to have Mankiewicz recalled as president. The recall ballot was pure DeMille; it permitted the "choice" of voting yes or not voting at all. The attempt at recall backfired, forcing the resignation of the SDG board of directors that included DeMille.[1]

However, it was not the liberal victory it seemed. The issue was not the loyalty oath as such (which the leading directors signed anyway) but DeMille's tyrannical methods. The times were not right for bucking a loyalty oath. Lillian Hellman refused to sign one for Harry Cohn at Columbia and found herself unemployable in Hollywood. Consequently, thirty-six directors took out an ad supporting Mankiewicz and also indicating that they "have signed the non-Communist loyalty oath required by the Guild," which was their way of being politically prudent and professionally humane. Even after the affair, Mankiewicz urged the SDG membership to sign the oath as a "voluntary act" of confidence in their union.

Still, it was courageous of Mankiewicz to take on a right-winger like DeMille. Although there seemed little likelihood of Mankiewicz's being

Cary Grant and Jeanne Crain as Dr. and Mrs. Noah Praetorius in People Will Talk. *(Credit: Margaret Herrick Library)*

blacklisted or subpoenaed to appear before the House Committee on Un-American Activities, he did write the dialogue for *Our Daily Bread* and produce *Fury*. If Jack Warner could call *Gentleman's Agreement* pro-Communist because it exposed American anti-Semitism, one wonders what he would have said about *No Way Out*.

People Will Talk (1951)

The DeMille imbroglio was an example of life mirroring—or, in this instance, sponsoring—art. Basically, it was a case of tyranny versus freedom which, coincidentally, was the theme of Mankiewicz's next film, *People Will Talk*. By 15 December 1950 Mankiewicz had prepared a 65-page treatment of Curt Goetz's play, *The Case of Dr. Praetorius*, in which the title character was an unconventional physician whose death in an auto accident led to the unearthing of some interesting facts. Praetorius believed he could be of greater service to his patients if they did not know he had a medical degree. Thus he worked as a cobbler so he could practice his own brand of medicine.

Mankiewicz only used the play's basic premise—Praetorius as miracle worker; he omitted the denouement explaining the circumstances of his death. When Praetorius asks his wife, who is in the car with him, why he could not find the microbe of human stupidity, she replies, "Because you are too stupid yourself, darling." Her response sends him into a fit of either laughter or tears and he crashes into a tree. Given Mankiewicz's penchant for black humor, he may have been tempted to retain the ending and construct a new plot around it. If he did, he would have had a clever one-liner for a conclusion and little else. By resisting the temptation, Mankiewicz made the only film of the McCarthy period about right-wing oppression without reference to Hollywood or Washington politics. While *High Noon* (1952) and *On the Waterfront* (1954) pitted the courage of the individual against apathy and corruption respectively, the townspeople of the former and the mob of the latter were neither right-wing nor self-righteous; and in neither film was the hero an intellectual under investigation.

The tension generated by the DeMille affair had abated, and Mankiewicz knew he would be resigning from the SDG presidency at the end of his first term. Thus he was in the mood to express his views on the human race, pouring them out so profusely in his first draft (15 February 1951) that Zanuck replied three days later, informing Mankiewicz that while people will talk, pictures must move. This will be "a very, very talky picture," Zanuck complained. Whether or not Zanuck realized it, his reaction to the draft gave the film its title which he changed from the one Mankiewicz preferred, *Doctor's Diary*, to *People Will Talk*—a title that could mean the kiss of death at the box office and, unfortunately, did.

As an example of the script's loquacity, Zanuck cited the unusually long prologue:

This will be part of the story of Noah Praetorius, M.D. There may be some who will claim to have identified Dr. Praetorius at once. There may be some who will reject the possibility that such a doctor lives, or could have lived. And there may be some who will hope that if he hasn't or doesn't, he certainly should. Our story is also—always with high regard—about medicine and the medical profession. Respectfully, therefore, with humble gratitude, the film is dedicated to one who has inspired man's unending battle against death, and without whom that battle is never won—The Patient.

Mankiewicz retained the prologue for which, one suspects, he had a certain fondness. Perhaps he believed there would be enough filmgoers who would see similarities between themselves and Praetorius's patients, Mankiewicz and Praetorius, and DeMille and the villain Elwell. However, just as one doubts that 1950s audiences interpreted *High Noon* as anti-McCarthy or *On the Waterfront* as Kazan's apologia for cooperating with HUAC, one doubts that many moviegoers saw themselves as patients cured by the healing hand of a moderate who challenged a tyrant and perhaps made it possible for them to see a few good films during the early fifties. More likely, they were pleased that Hollywood, after years of glorifying the doctor (*Magnificent Obsession*, 1935; *Disputed Passage*, 1939; the Dr. Kildare series, etc.), finally acknowledged the patient.

Although Mankiewicz got his way with the prologue (which was not a major victory), he yielded to Zanuck's judgment on the opening. The film was supposed to open with the dean's defending Praetorius against the charge of being an unorthodox teacher. Zanuck felt that if it opened on a defensive note, it would be advocating what it was supposed to be dramatizing. Nor would direction alone solve the problem: "What I refer to is a matter of dialogue mainly and characterization." The first draft was also didactic, with Praetorius sounding like a cross between a bore and a clown.

Zanuck was ambivalent about the screenplay. He must have sensed it would not result in a box-office hit; on the other hand, it would not be a costly production. He also knew that a Mankiewicz first draft tended to favor dialogue over action. Thus Zanuck exhorted him to keep the plot "moving" and protect himself with close-ups "so that we can make dialogue eliminations should they become essential. This happens in the best of scripts."

Zanuck's suggestions resulted in a genuinely witty opening. Mankiewicz introduced the villain and the villainess, Rodney Elwell (Hume Cronyn) and Miss Pickett (Margaret Hamilton), as unobtrusively as he introduced the Manleighs in *Wives*. Miss Pickett's visit to Elwell is motivated by her belief that Dr. Praetorius (Cary Grant), who is on the medical staff of the college where Elwell teaches anatomy, is her former employer—a butcher, known for his miraculous cures, who was run out of town when the people discovered that he worked wonders because he was a bona fide doctor.

The scene could easily have become conspiratorial and nasty since Hamilton tended to play busybodies in a particularly grating manner. Instead, Mankiewicz gave her fast quips and double entendres that allowed her to underplay rather than exaggerate. When Miss Pickett objects to Elwell's closing his office door, he remarks: "I've always conducted my affairs behind closed doors for twenty years," to which Miss Pickett replies immediately, without even a second for a double take, "Not with me." Elwell's rejoinder caps the exchange: "You overestimate both of us."

The opening also assured the audience it would not be subjected to political cant or liberal pieties. Although *People Will Talk* is a defense of the free thinker, it is also a paean to humanity and to what men like Dr. Praetorius do for it. The subject may recall Shaw's *The Doctor's Dilemma* (1906), but there is nothing Shavian about the film. If anything, it resembles Thurber and Nugent's *The Male Animal* (1940) as it might have been adapted by Philip Barry, adding his own special wit to the warmth and humor that were already present.

Zanuck objected to Praetorius's first being seen in a classroom, arguing with female students about sexism and spouting platitudes. Mankiewicz revised the scene so that, while Praetorius first appears in a lecture hall, he is neither a Mr. Chips nor an Immanuel Rath; he is the humanistic wit that most pre-med students dream of getting for their teacher. Standing next to a skeleton, Praetorius is man juxtaposed with his mortality. Yet he can joke about the skeleton, poking at the bones and noting, without belaboring the point, that an appreciation of the humanistic values of medicine begins when students realize the cadavers they dissect were human beings.

The classroom scene is important for another reason; during his lecture, one of the students, Deborah Higgins (Jeanne Crain), faints. She is pregnant, and Praetorius marries her not for the clichéd reason of giving her child a name, but because he wants to revive her faith in the essential goodness of life which children have an easier time accepting than adults. Therefore, he encourages cerebral types to put aside their tomes and play with electric trains. When Praetorius cannot prescribe, he comforts. In *People Will Talk*, there is a moment when poignancy and humor intermingle, rather like that unforgettable shot in *Cat on a Hot Tin Roof* (1958) when Elizabeth Taylor laughs and cries simultaneously. Praetorius stops at the bed of a terminally ill woman. After their chat, she says gratefully, "You certainly make dying a pleasure." If Mankiewicz were in a different mood, a blacker one, he might have faded out then. But Praetorius—and here Grant's delivery made all the difference between sincerity and cynicism—replies, "We'll keep that our little secret. I wouldn't want it to get around."

People Will Talk may not be the kind of movie one remembers for its unusual compositions; yet despite its emphasis on dialogue, it is never less than cinematic. The crosscutting at the end with Elwell trudging along in the night while within Praetorius conducts Brahms's Academic Festival Overture would be impossible in fiction, as would the visual contrasts Mankiewicz has so artfully worked out. Mankiewicz uses antithesis to highlight the differences between the moderates and the extremists. Both Elwell and Praetorius are associated with avatars of mortality. Elwell has a skull on his desk; Praetorius lectures alongside a skeleton. The skeleton is a human framework; the skull is a human artifact, a vestige of the medieval obsession with death. It would be more appropriate in a desert father's cell than on a professor's desk. Yet it represents exactly what Elwell is—head severed from body, reason dissociated from feeling.

Antithesis extends to the characterizations. Both Praetorius and Deborah's father, Arthur Higgins, are treated shabbily by the right-wingers. Praetorius is forced to testify about his past before Elwell's committee; Higgins, a failed intellectual, is forced to live with his uncultured brother.

Music is another means of contrast, a way of distinguishing the human from the subhuman. In *Wives*, music was the food of love; in *People Will Talk*, the concept is still Shakespearean, but the play is different. Although Mankiewicz never mentions *The Merchant of Venice*, one cannot help but think of Lorenzo's portrait of nonmusical man when one sees Elwell and Deborah's Uncle John: "The man that hath no music in himself, / Nor is not moved with concord of sweet sounds, / Is fit for treasons, stratagems and spoils; / The motions of his spirit are dull as night / And his affections dark as Erebus: Let no such man be trusted" (act 5, scene 2).

In the film, one of the most unlikely characters has music in him. It is Shunderson, Praetorius's Man Friday, played with a marvellously stolid dignity by Finlay Currie. Although he is dull-witted and a convicted murderer, as he explains in a monologue as humorous as it is moving, he more than makes up for what he lacks in intelligence by a superabundance of humanity. In a scene that epitomizes the inner harmony that music brings, Shunderson listens, thoroughly relaxed, to the Prize Song from *Die Meistersinger von Nürnberg* (1868), the noblest of Wagner's music dramas. Uncle John, on the other hand, scoffs at anything pertaining to the mind, preferring radio programs to classical music. However, he does purport to live by the Bible. To deepen the contrast between John Higgins and Shunderson, Mankiewicz gives each of them a dog. Higgins has a grim hound called Beelzebub; Shunderson, a gentle collie that resembles Lassie.

People Will Talk celebrates the triumph of the spirit over forces that would enslave it, including nature itself. Early in the film, Praetorius extols the days of butter in the tub and sauerkraut in the barrel; but he is not advocating a return to prelapsarian times. "Old mother nature," he argues, "tries to destroy mankind periodically with pestilence and disease. That's why the human race has been at war with old mother nature ever since it became the human race." What Praetorius is arguing for is not a belief in physical nature but in *natura naturans*, nature conceived of as a creative force—as a form of God.

A celebration requires music, and Mankiewicz ends the film with a composition that makes the spine stiffen with pride: the Academic Festival Overture, whose coda is the famous student song, *Gaudeamus Igitur*, here sung by a chorus. As Praetorius conducts triumphantly, Mankiewicz cuts to Elwell, "the man that hath no music in himself," walking under the archway and looking smaller than usual after his defeat. But inside, the music swells into an affirmation of everything the film stands for—the invincibility of the human spirit. As the chorus praises *alma mater*, the song becomes a hymn to something that, until now, remained in the background: the university which, literally, is predicated upon one goal—the perfection of humankind. The finale is also Mankiewicz's tribute to the teaching profession, his father's profession, which he now makes the subject of a musical tribute.

Since Mankiewicz knows his Latin, he can crack a learned joke. At the point in *Gaudeamus Igitur*, when the chorus sings "Vivat membrum quod libet / vivant membra quae libet" ("Long live each and every member"—that is, of the university), Deborah feels the child stir within her. If one thinks the timing is accidental, one is underestimating Mankiewicz's intelligence.

The Quiet American (1958)

The Quiet American was the reverse of *People Will Talk* which, although it never specified sides (except the side of the human race), excluded the Elwells of the world who closed their windows to the sound of music. In Mankiewicz's adaptation of Graham Greene's 1955 novel, *The Quiet American*, the sides—or rather the side— is as clear as De Mille's recall ballot which only allowed for a vote of yes. On Mankiewicz's *Quiet American* ballot, one votes American or not at all. This, however, was not the case in Greene's novel which took place toward the end of the first Indochina War. One must remember, first, that Greene, who in the early 1950s made four trips to Indochina as a war correspondent, set the action of the novel in 1952, two years before the United States committed itself to supporting the French war effort there;[2] second, that he published the novel in 1955, shortly after Dien Bien Phu marked the end of French rule in Indochina and the real beginning of American involvement in Vietnam, of which Greene was sharply critical. Although Greene made the title character symbolic of misguided American intervention, he did not vilify the American; he merely presented him as ideologically naive and politically dangerous. The "quiet American" was Alden Pyle, the Princeton-educated son of a college professor, who came to Saigon to ally himself with General The because he was attracted to The's idea of a third force—an independent Vietnam that was neither Communist nor French.

It might be tempting to regard Pyle as the villain except that, intellectually, he is incapable of villainy. Pyle is an inveterate do-gooder, a theorist without an original idea, a prude. Pyle no sooner meets Fowler, the British war correspondent, than he woos away Fowler's Anamite mistress, Phuong, a symbol of a tragically docile Vietnam. Therefore, Fowler does not thwart a Communist attempt to assassinate Pyle, although he pleads with the American to dissociate himself from The, using British colonialism as an example of the destructiveness of misplaced zeal. When Pyle persists, Fowler makes no effort to save him.

It was part of Greene's purpose to show the similarity between personal and political intervention. Fowler knows from experience the futility of meddling in a country's internal affairs. Pyle is just "ignorant and silly and . . . got involved." He is the guileless fool of mythology who pays for his folly. Even Vigot, the Catholic police inspector, admits that Pyle "was doing a lot of harm."

Although Greene was drawing on firsthand experience, Mankiewicz thought that the novel was unduly anti-American. Therefore, the film discreetly avoided connecting General The with acts of terrorism; yet when Greene was in Saigon he heard about bombings that were attributed to The and his followers—plastic charges in vehicles and explosives in bicycle pumps. But how did The acquire these explosives? And how did he learn to use them in such a sophisticated way? There were "rumours that The had acquired his 'know-how' from agents of the American Central Intelligence Bureau who, in their desire to promote a third force, had provided the Cao Dai Colonel with some technical assistance in addition to moral support."[3]

Although Greene made no connection between Pyle and the CIA, Pyle could easily pass for a CIA recruit. However, it is clear that Pyle is working for General The, who in 1952 founded the National Resistance Front for the purpose of forming a Vietnamese nationalist army as part of his attempt to achieve autonomy for Vietnam. Pyle's attraction to The is understandable. The was uncommonly moral, although he might have been bribed to support Diem because of Diem's success in fighting communism. As a champion of freedom, Pyle would favor anyone advocating self-determination. Still, one would like to know what Pyle does besides back General The. In the novel, one is never quite sure. "People say he imports a great many things," Phuong remarks to Fowler. Among those imports is plastic. "You don't mean bombs?" Fowler asks. "No. Just plastic," she replies.

According to Kenneth Geist, Mankiewicz believed Greene erred in his use of the term "plastic," confusing the popular meaning with the explosive that, in French, is called *le plastic*; and, in English, is sometimes referred to as plastique (for example, C4 plastique). To correct Greene and absolve the American from any implication in The's terrorism, Mankiewicz had him importing plastic—"American plastic," as the script carefully indicates—for toy-making. In the film, the Communists trick Fowler into thinking the American is importing explosives for The; thus Fowler's cooperation in the American's murder becomes the act of a jealous lover who rids himself of a rival.

Since Greene is bilingual, he obviously knew the difference between plastique and plastic; between *le plastic* and *les matières plastiques*, "plastic goods": "The plastic in *The Quiet American* was not explosive. It was a plastic from which the containers of the bicycle bombs in the form of bicycle pumps was made. Not the actual bomb itself."[4]

The issue was far less important than Mankiewicz or Geist thought. Greene introduced the bicycle pump bombs because they were part of The's terrorist campaign. The difference between the novel and the film is that Greene's American knew how the plastic would be used (as containers for the explosives) while Mankiewicz's American planned to use the plastic to manufacture toys for the Chinese New Year, thus performing the ultimate goodwill gesture by bringing toyland to Saigon.

To fashion a pro-American, anti-Communist film from a novel that was anti-American but neutral on the matter of communism, Mankiewicz had to make the title character the embodiment of American morality—an American everyman. Consequently, Mankiewicz does not give him a name which makes introductions awkward since Fowler must keep referring to the "young American." But there was another problem with the character; Mankiewicz seemed to have little sympathy for him. While Mankiewicz may have believed in the American's anticommunism, he did not believe in the American who, as played by Audie Murphy with a spooky sincerity, cannot command belief. Murphy did not so much reflect the mentality of the Cold War; he was the Cold War.

Structurally, at least, Mankiewicz was faithful to Greene, reproducing the novel's first-person narration through his favorite technique of the flashback with periodic voice-over. Mankiewicz also retained some of Greene's dialogue which he sometimes reassigned. When Fowler notes that Phuong means Phoenix, the American explains what a phoenix is for those who have never had a course in mythology. In the novel, Fowler gave the explanation which was more appropriate; it is hard to imagine the American's taking courses in anything except ethics and political science.

Given Murphy's characterization of the American as not so much anti-intellectual as nonintellectual, one also wonders how he could identify the passage from *Othello* (act 3, scene 3) that Fowler reads aloud at the window—a sign to the assassins that the American would be meeting him at a local restaurant later that evening. In the novel, Fowler read a poem by Arthur Hugh Clough. However, Mankiewicz is stressing Fowler's jealousy, the *locus classicus* for which is *Othello.* Thus the

Audie Murphy wooing Giorgia Moll away from her British love in The Quiet American. *(Courtesy: United Artists)*

manner of betrayal coincides with the motive; the medium is the message. By using *Othello*, Mankiewicz can connect the themes of political involvement and personal jealousy; ultimately, Fowler betrays the American because the American has alienated Phuong from him. The American's interference in Vietnamese affairs is insignificant compared to his disruption of Fowler's love life.

However, as played by Michael Redgrave in one of his finest screen performances, Fowler seems almost justified in taking any measures he can to win back Phuong. What the American feels for Phuong is an infatuation with the exotic; Fowler knows that convergence of passion and tenderness which, if it is not love, is what often passes for it. Mankiewicz went much further than Greene in his characterization of Fowler. What Greene concealed behind a façade of reserve and detachment, Mankiewicz stripped away to reveal a man torn between the apathy he cultivated and the faith he wished he had; between the vindication of his manhood and a gentlemanly admission of defeat. Fowler is one of Mankiewicz's most complex characters. However, like his character, Mankiewicz was similarly divided. As a screenwriter, he was attracted primarily to Fowler; as an American who was piqued by an anti-American novel (which he also found carelessly written), he wanted to deflect any sympathy away from Fowler and toward the American.

But it did not work. One feels Fowler's loss more deeply than the American's death, if one feels the American's death at all. Mankiewicz has gone out of his way to make Fowler suffer for his complicity in the assassination, even invoking the old Hays Office principle of retribution. In the novel, Fowler not only gets Phuong back; he also learns that his wife has agreed to a divorce. In the film, after hearing the news of the divorce, he tracks Phuong down in a nightclub, only to have her denounce him as uncaring and concerned only with his next pipe—a line that is meaningless unless one has read the novel in which Phuong was especially adept at preparing his opium pipe. Rebuffed by his former mistress, Fowler is even more pitiable and, despite the retributive ending, more sympathetic.

What Mankiewicz has done, perhaps intentionally, is give Fowler a sense of guilt that places him in the tradition of Greene's Catholic protagonists like the priest in *The Power and the Glory* (1940) and Scobie in *The Heart of the Matter* (1948). Greene's Fowler was not a Catholic, nor was Mankiewicz's—in the denominational sense. But spiritually he was, evoking the tortured Catholics in Greene's plays *The Living Room* (1953) and *The Potting Shed* (1957). In the last line of the novel, Fowler expressed only the slightest pang of regret: "Everything had gone right with me since he had died, but how I wished there existed someone to whom I could say that I was sorry." Mankiewicz cut the first part of the line, but even "I wished there existed someone to whom I could say that I was sorry" is not the fade-out. In response to Fowler's desire to purge himself, Vigot (Claude Dauphin) makes a suggestion: "I drive past the Cathedral." But Fowler, looking as haunted as Orestes hounded by the furies, turns away and disappears into the night.

The confusion between politics and passion in the film might have been less apparent if Mankiewicz did not include references, however oblique, to Diem. Mankiewicz made *The Quiet American* after South Vietnam became a republic with Diem as president. In the film, the American is about to give up on General The as the hope of the third force and transfer his allegiance to an unnamed "prominent Vietnamese" living in exile in New Jersey whom he had met while doing graduate work at Princeton; and who, when Vietnam became an independent republic, would be the mean between colonialism and communism. Although the movie, like the novel, is set in 1952, Mankiewicz's end title, a note of thanks "to the people of the republic of Vietnam and their chosen president," requires one to view the film as a prelude to the creation of the Diem government.

Looking at *The Quiet American* in light of the fall of Saigon in 1975, one realizes that the president Mankiewicz thanked was Diem who was "chosen" through an election in which 450,000 voters cast 605,000 ballots and whose brutally repressive methods led to his assassination in 1963. Yet the novel and the film have one note in common: each was prophetic in its own way. The novel warned what would happen if an America, as symbolized by Alden Pyle, backed a right-wing government in an effort to keep Vietnam from going Communist. The film was an endorsement of that government to whose survival the United States committed itself. However, it was a commitment that led to widespread disaffection among the young who, in the 1960s, discovered that the alternative to being a hawk was being a dove; and that compromise meant joining the counterculture or settling in Canada.

Carol for Another Christmas (1964)

Carol for Another Christmas, Mankiewicz's only venture into television directing, pushed beyond the right-wing boundaries of *The Quiet American* into liberal country; not back to the world of *People Will Talk* where the purple mountains still had their majesty, but into an America where that majesty was lost to the mushroom cloud and where the fruited plain was scorched by the fires of Hiroshima. Although the script was written by Rod Serling, Mankiewicz seemed to have been sympathetic to his portrayal of an America wracked by bigotry and dissension. Perhaps the fact that Serling wrote the script shortly after President Kennedy's assassination contributed to its bleakness.

The project was sponsored by the Telsun Foundation which was created to produce and distribute, in addition to *Carol, Who Has Seen the Wind?* (1965) and *Once upon a Tractor* (1965), all of which argued for human rights and peaceful coexistence and, in general, reflected United Nations ideals. *Carol,* which ABC aired on 28 December 1964, was an updating of Dickens's *A Christmas Carol* in which the Scrooge figure, now called Daniel Grudge (Sterling Hayden), is a conservative bigot who shocks his liberal nephew (Ben Gazzara) by vetoing a cultural exchange at the local college because it will mean playing host to a professor from a Communist country. "There's only one side I'm on," Grudge boasts; "our side." On Christmas Eve, he has a vision, a dream, or a hallucination (one is uncertain) that at least is imaginatively introduced by the tinkling prisms of the chandelier. Grudge encounters the ghost of Christmas past as a GI; the ghost of Christmas present as a glutton who gorges himself while displaced persons hover in a barbwire compound; and the ghost of Christmas future who ushers him into a bombed out town hall where the "me generation" has assembled for a meeting presided over by the Imperial Me (Peter Sellers), a parody of Lyndon Johnson with his ten-gallon hat and "Perfect Society of the I" program. The town meeting scene culminates in a child's whipping out a pistol and shooting a black who is pleading for brotherhood.

There was little Mankiewicz could do with such an unsubtle script; the need for close-ups that television demanded militated against any interesting *mise-en-scène,* as did the low budget that was reflected in the sets. There was one Mankiewicz touch, however. The town hall resembled the drum in *Suddenly, Last Summer* with the spaced-out Americans acting like the mental patients in the film.

Carol was aired only once; it was never repeated because of opposition from the DAR and the John Birch Society. Yet, in its way, it was as intellectually demeaning as anti-Communist propaganda like *My Son John* (1952). *Carol* made one feel guilty for being alive; since Serling covered all possibilities, this meant being alive in the prewar past, the postwar present, or the nuclear future. There was no "God bless us, every one" because there was no Tiny Tim; there was only the United Nations children's chorus caroling over the radio as a chastened Grudge eats his Christmas breakfast in the kitchen like a true American.

Carol was worthy of neither Serling nor Mankiewicz. The fact that it can be viewed only at the United Nations indicates its origins and purpose. The UN will survive it.

7

Commoners, Countesses, and Carnivores

Five Fingers (1952)

ON THE SURFACE *Five Fingers* seemed a strange choice for Mankiewicz: a spy thriller about a British ambassador's valet who sold classified information to the Nazis toward the close of World War II. Yet Mankiewicz always had a flair for the theatrical; and the corkscrew plot of *Five Fingers* had so many twists that it seemed more like a stage melodrama than an espionage tale. If, as Michael Rennie observes in the film, "counterespionage is the highest form of gossip," then espionage itself is another form of theater, with the degree of theatricality determined by the way the cloak and dagger devices are used: the assumption of the code name; assignations after dark; bargains struck in doorways with each negotiation becoming a scene, and each scene a link in a chain of events that brings the scenario to its climax.

Five Fingers was also a property that would appeal to Zanuck, who continued to fight World War II cinematically long after it was over—from the triumph of *The Longest Day* (1962) to the disaster of *Tora! Tora! Tora!* (1970). It was clear that Zanuck had more to say about World War II even in the early and mid 1950s when Fox made a number of major films that were either set during the war (*Twelve O'Clock High*, 1949; *Halls of Montezuma*, 1950; *Decision before Dawn*, 1951) or in postwar Europe (*Diplomatic Courier*, 1952; *Night People*, 1954). *Five Fingers* was released the year after *Decision before Dawn*, with which it shared certain characteristics. Both involved spies with code names, one of whom is working on his own and dubbed Cicero (*Five Fingers*); the other, recruited by the Americans and known as Happy (*Decision before Dawn*). Both had a semidocumentary format with periodic voice-over narration, an opening title attesting to the authenticity of locales, and credits appearing against a plain background.

James Mason as Diello, the valet-spy, in Five Fingers—*a title that has no connection with the plot. (Credit: Margaret Herrick Library)*

101

Both films purported to be historically accurate, as the opening titles reminded us. However, *Five Fingers* eased the burden that truth imposes on moviegoers by following the declaration with a precredits sequence, striking the right note of theatricality. An M.P. rises in the House of Commons, brandishing a book, entitled *Operation Cicero*, that documents a case of espionage in the British embassy at Ankara in 1944. The foreign secretary replies that the book is indeed accurate and that every precaution is being taken so that the situation it portrays will never recur. A "This is a true story" title then appears, followed by the credits accompanied by Bernard Herrmann's spidery score.

The music playfully undermines the claim of authenticity, implying that even if it is a true story, the movie is going to be fun. The off-camera voice that introduces the first scene also tries to be serious, but it cannot suppress its sense of irony. The sound of war is in the distance; close by is the sound of Wagner. We are at a diplomatic reception where a soprano is belting out Brünnhilde's battle cry from *Die Walküre* (1870) as if she were trying to deflect a falling bomb. Off in a corner, out of earshattering range, is the Countess Staviska (Danielle Darrieux); her plate piled high with buffet food that she consumes like the hungry aristocrat that she is, never letting manners interfere with her appetite and never letting anyone bring her champagne when she can have beer. When the countess offers her services to Reichsambassador Franz von Papen, he politely refuses, knowing that the countess's allegiance is exclusively to herself. In 1939, the countess, christened Anna, left Poland for purely practical reasons: "Bombs were falling. I thought I would be in the way."

The opening scene has set the tone of the film. One is in the world of the drawing room and the salon where life is lived as theater and people converse in repartee; where everything is high—the intrigue, the melodrama, the comedy. With the alliance of Anna and Diello (James Mason), the spy who had once been her husband's valet, Mankiewicz was able to return to his favorite theme—the tension between the commoner and the aristocrat.

However, when the aristocrat is a countess and the commoner a valet, there is always the possibility that a battle of the sexes might ensue or that a Lady Chatterley–Mellors situation might develop. Either turn of events would be inappropriate in a thriller which, nominally, is what *Five Fingers* is. Thus Mankiewicz must weave the theme into the fabric of the espionage tale which he does quite effectively. Diello visits the countess in her shabby flat, offering her a way out of her present impoverishment. Diello needs someone to deposit the money he receives from the sale of government secrets. His willingness to provide her with a palatial home is also motivated by expediency: he needs a place for his transactions. But it is not merely a business proposition

Diello is making to Anna. He wants her to regard him as an equal, something she is loath to do. Anna may have fallen upon hard times, but she has not fallen into egalitarian ways.

There are three scenes between Diello and Anna—two in her flat, one in the drawing room of the rented house—that are staged with an artistry revealing Mankiewicz at his peak as he captures every suppressed thought and repressed feeling, every nuance of expression and sign of tension that occur when one person momentarily steps out of the role in which society has cast him, while the other continues to follow the scenario.

There is an air of fatalistic languor hanging over the first scene. The flat is seedy; clothes are strewn about; and Anna's attitude is one of bored resignation. The phonograph plays two records, presumably the extent of her collection: *Adieu, mon coeur* and *Mon ami*, sung dreamily, smokily by a chanteuse who sounds more worldly wise than Piaf, but not so vulnerable. One will hear these songs again. With psychological shrewdness, as if he had entered Diello's consciousness, Mankiewicz has Diello stand over Anna as she sits at her dressing table, suggesting that now, for the first time, he has the upper hand. But Diello does not revel in her misfortune; always the valet, he even tidies up. When Anna requests a brandy, Diello obliges and also pours one for himself. Just when he thinks he has succeeded in removing the social barrier between them, Anna rebuffs him: "I shall drink only out of one glass, thank you." Dutifully, Diello pours the contents of the second glass back into the bottle.

But he has not given up. Without gloating like an operatic villain, he reminds Anna that, with his money, she could redeem her jewels and move to more dignified surroundings. He then adds that he knows she will never divulge the source of the money because she would be too embarrassed to admit it came from her husband's ex-valet. Anna takes her cue from Diello's proposition which, without being blatantly obvious, has made it clear who is indebted to whom. Diello also admits that, in making the offer, he has treated her as an inferior; their relationship must be on her terms. At that point, Mankiewicz does something quite interesting: he frames the two of them together on the sofa, looking as if they are equals; but only as business partners. Once that is understood, they can move to a first-name basis. "My name is Anna," the countess says, taking pencil and paper. "Now let's get down to business."

In the second scene, Diello's fortunes are in the ascendant. He puffs on a cigar with entrepreneurial satisfaction. Not a slicked down hair is out of place, and his dressing gown fits like tailored apparel. Anna is resplendent in a black rhinestone-studded gown; they look like equals: a gentleman (as opposed to a gentleman's gentleman) and his lady. But that equality is deceptive; Diello is now making a bid for supremacy. After he describes his plan to settle in Rio de Janeiro on the money he will shortly have, Anna, who reacts instinctively to big bucks, kisses him passionately, thus losing her beloved status. Now Diello can say, "Get me a drink"; and Anna must fetch it. But like everything else about Anna, her acquiescence is insincere.

Each of the Anna–Diello scenes is a variation on the theme of class conflict. In the first, they progress from superior and inferior to temporary equals; in the second, from temporary equals to superior and inferior; now, they are back where they were at the beginning. In their last scene together, they are in the dingy flat again. Anna has procured passports for them under the names of Signor and Signora Antonini; like children, they playact at being husband and wife. One is almost touched by their restored innocence, but the restoration is only temporary. When Diello asks Anna if she will miss being a countess, she replies, "Not for a moment." As they embrace, the camera lingers on her face which is no longer suffused with girlish ebullience but taut with cunning, mocking the emotion it had so successfully feigned.

Anna double-crosses Diello by absconding to Switzerland and sending two letters—one to the British ambassador, claiming that Diello was a German agent; and another to von Papen, claiming he was a British plant. It is not that Anna is trying to cover herself; she is, after all, moving from neutral Turkey to neutral Switzerland as one would expect of someone who is apolitical, apathetic, and amoral. Anna believes in settling scores. She punishes Diello for presuming he could enter her class; she now punishes von Papen for rejecting her services. When the head of German intelligence discovers Diello was working for the British, he hurls the last documents the Nazis had purchased from him out the window, assuming they are fraudulent; actually, they were the plans for the Normandy invasion.

Mankiewicz uses the act of throwing away seemingly useless paper to build a three-part sequence in which the gesture progresses from a symbol of lost love, to one of lost dominion, and culminates as a symbol of the lost dream. The subtle joining of scenes through images (paper), repeated dialogue (a request for a drink), or repeated music (the French love songs) has always characterized sophisticated filmmaking. Hitchcock was always building sequences imagistically or thematically; in *Notorious* (1946) he used a bottle of champagne to unify three separate scenes. In *Five Fingers* Mankiewicz did the same with paper.

In his train compartment, en route to Istanbul, Diello reads Anna's letter to the British ambassador that accuses him of being a German spy. He tears it up, tossing the pieces out of the train window—his face masking the emotion that his profession does not allow him to express. When von Richter hurls the Normandy plans out of the window, they blow in the direction of the ship that is taking Diello to Rio—a trip they helped to finance. At the end of the film, Diello repeats the same gesture in a similarly ironic context.

Ensconced in a villa overlooking the ocean, Diello is dining in style, wearing the white dinner jacket he coveted when he was a cabin boy. A bank official and a member of the Brazilian Department of Investigation interrupt his solitary meal; it seems the money he deposited in the local bank is worthless. Diello had asked to be paid for his services in British pounds which von Richter warned him would be worthless once Germany won the war. But even though Germany lost, they are still worthless because they are counterfeit. When Diello learns that the same counterfeit money turned up in Switzerland in the possession of a female political prisoner, he cries, "Anna!" Laughing, he tosses the useless notes over the railing. Although double-crossed twice, Diello has not lost his sense of humor.

There are really two revelations in the final scene, the most obvious being the duplicity of the Nazis. But *Five Fingers* has a cumulative power; at its close, one has learned something that brings together the themes of class distinction, espionage, and Diello's dream of the good life. What one learns at the end is that Anna is Diello's double, his lower form. That realization grows progressively during the film until it acquires the force of an epiphany. They are not doubles just because they were both victims of Nazi treachery and of a scheme that backfired. In the last scene, when Diello is finishing dinner, we hear the same music we heard in Anna's flat—those languid *chansons*. It is hardly the kind of music that goes with white dinner jackets and vintage wines. But then, Anna also had a penchant for beer and cold cuts.

Viewed as a double, Diello is Anna's superior. Doubles are never equal. The shadow is not equal to the one who casts it; Mr. Hyde is not superior to Henry Jekyll. What makes Diello Anna's superior is the fact that whatever success he enjoyed was the result of work; with Anna, it was a matter of luck. Anna was not born into royalty; she merely happened to marry a Polish count. Anna fell into good fortune; Diello worked at achieving it. While both of them could serve either the Axis or the Allies, Diello can at least be contemptuous of the Nazis to whom he sells Allied secrets, although he has no pangs of conscience about what he does. Selling information is not the same as selling the ability to use it, he argues. It was fitting that the Germans gave him the code name of Cicero, "a man of nobility, eloquence, and dissatisfaction," Diello observes, pleased at being associated with the Roman orator and statesman. Cicero was never one of the nobility, but a *novus homo* or "new man" from a family whose members had never held a magistracy; in short, a man not unlike Diello.

Since Diello is not fortune's child, one accepts him as someone striving to improve his station in life. In fact, one wants him to succeed and enjoy the good life in Rio; he deserves it. It is hard to dismiss the skill with which he opens safes and the professionalism with which he photographs documents. To Diello, espionage is an extension of his duties as valet—an avocation he pursues with formidable efficiency. But espionage is also a business. When he receives his final payment from Moyzisch, the jittery go-between, he says: "I suppose a gentleman would not count the money; but unfortunately, I will not be a gentleman until after I've finished counting it"; which he does with a bank teller's dexterity, making the notes crackle under his practiced fingers. That he can elude both the Germans and the British points to something more than mere ingenuity. Surely a villa in Rio is not an unreasonable wish.

James Mason's performance contributed greatly to audience sympathy for Diello. Having created the tragic Rommel the year before in *The Desert Fox* (1951), he would follow *Five Fingers* with another paradoxical character, "the noblest Roman of them all"—Brutus in Mankiewicz's *Julius Caesar* (1953). Mason imparted a measure of nobility to every role he played from the highwayman of *The Wicked Lady* (1945) to the nympholept of *Lolita* (1962). Danielle Darrieux gave Anna an air of amorality that was so fitting it almost seemed right. One thought of Anna as one of Dante's neutrals who stood for nothing. Here was an instance of life imitating art. Alida Valli was originally slated for Anna. However, with Darrieux the role takes on unique political overtones. When Anna offers her services to the Third Reich, one thinks of Danielle Darrieux, the World War II collaborationist, whose activities are documented in Marcel Ophuls's *The Sorrow and the Pity* (1972). While Diello conformed to Mason's screen image, Anna reflected Darrieux's wartime role.

The core of *Five Fingers* is Diello's attempt to rise above his class. Whether a 1972 audience or even one viewing it today would see class distinction as the theme uniting all the others is problematical. Yet it is Diello's desire to transcend his class that motivates his trafficking in espionage, his alliance with Anna, and his escape to Rio. Since Mankiewicz's best films work on more than one level, a viewer can simply enjoy *Five Fingers* as an exercise in suspense. However, the suspense that Mankiewicz generated would have been impossible unless someone had first gutted the source, L. C. Moyzisch's *Operation Cicero* (1950). Moyzisch, who appears in the film as the go-between, was an attaché at the German embassy in Ankara. As soon as he published his memoir, the studios recognized its film potential, with Fox outbidding MGM, Alexander Korda, and J. Arthur Rank for the rights.

The screenplay is attributed to Michael Wilson, the left-wing screenwriter who was blacklisted in 1952 for taking the Fifth Amendment when he was questioned by the House Committee on Un-American Activities about his communist past. Although Mankiewicz rewrote Wilson's dialogue, he did not share screen credit with Wilson; Zanuck agreed to make the film on the condition that Mankiewicz's contribution to the script would be uncredited.

Wilson and Mankiewicz were dealing with a book that had no conclusion. Moyzisch did not know what happened to Cicero; he only knew that Cicero wanted to build "a large house in some paradisaical part of the globe where there were no Englishmen." Wilson and Mankiewicz specified the location of the paradise, making it the fulfillment of a boyhood dream. While Moyzisch acknowledged that most of the money Cicero received was counterfeit, Wilson and Mankiewicz had to dramatize the repercussions of the swindle. They used the memoir only for some characters (Moyzisch, Cicero, von Papen) and the plot peg. There was no Countess Staviska in *Operation Cicero*; Moyzisch's secretary who defects to the British does not even come close. And above all, the memoir had no wit. In the movie, Diello tosses off aphorisms that may not as yet have found their place in film's dictionary of phrase and fable. But there is a worthy candidate, a line spun on the wheel of sarcasm but honed on the whetstone of wit: "When you die, Hitler will dip you in bronze and name streets after you" (Diello to Moyzisch). "Fasten your seatbelts. It's going to be a bumpy night" seems almost tame by comparison.

The Barefoot Contessa (1954)

The Barefoot Contessa was the logical successor to *Five Fingers*; here, the commoner turns into a countess. But even before Maria Vargas (Ava Gardner) became the Contessa Torlato-Favrini, she felt inferior to no one. In fact, her earth-sprung beauty made commoners of royalty. However, the film is never viewed this way; *The Barefoot Contessa* is usually considered Mankiewicz's "Hollywood film," as *Sunset Boulevard* (1950) was Billy Wilder's and *The Bad and the Beautiful* (1952) was Vincente Minnelli's. While *The Barefoot Contessa* portrays the creation of a star, it is also quite different from any other film about filmmaking. Only a brief part of the action takes place in Hollywood; most of it is set in Madrid, Rome, and the Italian Riviera. If anything, the film evokes the postwar movie industry that looked for Mediterranean beauties like Silvana Mangano, Sophia Loren, Rosanna Podesta, and

"Earth-Sprung Beauty"—Director Harry Dawes (Humphrey Bogart) discovers the barefoot contessa (Ava Gardner) in Spain. (Credit: Movie Star News)

Gina Lollobrigida—an industry that was developing a jet set *la dolce vita* image as deals were negotiated on yachts instead of in posh restaurants or around swimming pools.

The Barefoot Contessa, Mankiewicz's first film as producer, director, and screenwriter, is also his most personal. It is his *Citizen Kane*, told, like Welles's film, from several points of view. It also represents his reflections at midcareer, taking him back to *Dragonwyck* where he first portrayed the impact of the aristocrat's world on a proletarian type. By a kind of artistic androgyny, Mankiewicz became one with his two main characters: Maria and writer-director Harry Dawes (Humphrey Bogart); with the creation and the creator, the star and the starmaker. By this double identification, Mankiewicz could explore the circular nature of stardom and the paradox that the starmaker is the star-made. For stardom depends as much on the transforming power of the starmaker as it does on the star's ability to be transformed. Having depicted the tension between the commoner and the aristocrat in a series of films, Mankiewicz was able to resolve it by dramatizing a paradox peculiar to the movies where commoners—and most movie stars were just that—

become royalty and, in turn, confer a similar distinction on the filmmaker who effects the transformation.

This is a noble idea, and it is fitting that, when *The Barefoot Contessa* opens, the titles should have a noble appearance: Roman letters carved on a sky-blue background. The accompanying music has a Mediterranean vitality, surging but not lush; in a quieter, more nostalgic form, it will become Maria's theme. Mankiewicz again uses a framing device, Maria's funeral. The camera tracks down the path to a crowd of mourners with umbrellas. However, one of the mourners does not have an umbrella; he is Harry Dawes, the chief narrator: "My name is Harry Dawes. I go way back—back to when the movies had two dimensions, and one dimension, and sometimes no dimension at all." As did Joseph L. Mankiewicz.

Noting that it was the kind of funeral Maria would want, Harry provides the cue for the first flashback, as the scene dissolves to a Madrid nightclub three years earlier. Maria is the club's main attraction, but one does not see her performance; only the castanets that she clicks. Harry, the exemplary host, introduces everyone at the table. First, Kirk Edwards, who is producing his first film—a teetotaler, a prude, and an ignoramus who knows nothing about *Faust* and needs a plot synopsis from Harry. Then there is Myrna, the blonde who's been around; and finally, the sweaty publicist Oscar Muldoon (Edmond O'Brien).

Edwards wants to be a starmaker, but Maria will not shine for him. Nor will she accept Muldoon's invitation to join them, answering through her dressing room door that she does not sit with customers. While she is indifferent to producers and contemptuous of their publicists, she is quite responsive to writer-directors and is willing to speak with Harry. She knows his work and that of other directors—Ernst Lubitsch, Victor Fleming, Woody Van Dyke, Gregory La Cava. One could speculate indefinitely on the significance these names have to Mankiewicz, but the point is that Maria knows the men who made the movies. Furthermore, she believes that the writer is more important than the producer. Consequently, Maria is Harry's alter ego, just as every Galatea is Pygmalion's; and just as Maria-Harry is Mankiewicz's.

Mythic Structure. While a studio head may try to superimpose a preconceived image upon a star, a writer-director knows that there is always some area within the star that resists transformation. In Maria's case it was her origins, symbolized by her desire to be barefoot. Significantly, before Harry meets Maria he first sees her bare feet. Being barefoot is all she has left of her innocence. It was only during the Spanish Civil War, when she pressed herself against the earth and burrowed her toes into the soil, that she wanted shoes. Otherwise, they were part of her dancing costume, not part of her.

Bogart's Harry Dawes is not unlike Joseph L. Mankiewicz.
(Credit: Margaret Herrick Library)

The Barefoot Contessa blends the Pygmalion and Galatea myth with the Cinderella story so successfully that both appear to be embedded in the plot rather than woven into it. However, the film is also a reinterpretation of the Cinderella story which itself deals with a split character: Ella of the cinders and the beloved of Prince Charming. Maria describes herself as half in the dirt and half out of it, torn between innocence and experience, between her roots and her aspirations. But unlike Cinderella, Maria cannot resolve her twin selves. Cinderella could because the prince brought her the glass slipper which made the transition possible. But Maria wants to walk barefoot. However, as an international star she does not have that luxury. As the Cinderella of the cinema she must conform to the scenario and inhabit a world of villas and yachts.

Her first prince is an Argentinian tycoon. When she boards his yacht, a close-up shows her wearing shoes. The dirt that once gave security to her shoeless feet has become moral rot. Cinderella is about to become a whore. At first, she is modest in her bathing suit; then she drops her bathrobe and falls on the mattress. When the Argentinian accuses her of being an animal without passion, it is his way of stating what she has already said of herself: that she was half in the dirt and half out of it, that she was spirit and matter—but in opposition, not in coalescence. Maria can never be totally mythic or completely real. Just when she thinks she has found reality in her marriage to the count (Rossano Brazzi), he tells her with great delicacy on their wedding night that he is impotent. Cinderella then becomes an earth mother, taking a lover to produce a child for her husband. But the count, ignorant of her motive, kills her and, in so doing, provides her with her last mythic role—the slain goddess.

Narrative Structure. Like many of his films, *The Barefoot Contessa* is flashback with voice-over narration. Harry is the main narrator but not the only one; Muldoon and the count supplement his account. Since Mankiewicz is using a fairly strict type of "I narration," the narrators are limited pretty much to what they have actually witnessed. Thus, Muldoon narrates the yacht trip since Harry was not on board; the count, the time he saw Maria in the gypsy camp since no one else was around. Multiple flashbacks do not disturb the film's mythic quality, although they do not enhance it, either. The flashbacks do not mesh as harmoniously as they did in *All about Eve*, in which three characters also remembered the same person. By restricting point of view to what a character would empirically know, Mankiewicz had to repeat part of a flashback as well as incorporate a flashback within a flashback. Muldoon's flashback ends with an incident in a casino where one of the patrons strikes the Argentinian for insulting Maria; the patron is later identified as the count. Muldoon ends his segment by observing that this was the last time he saw Maria, who would die as the Contessa Torlato-Favrini. Immediately, the scene shifts to the gravesite as the count takes up the story, describing the first time he saw Maria, dancing in the gypsy camp, barefoot and uninhibited. It is the most memorable scene in the movie and the most pictorial in any Mankiewicz film. The music combines the proud measures of a Spanish air with a sensuous nobility; Maria dances to it as if she had been released from a painting and was rediscovering the joy of freedom.

Thus Maria was not unknown to the count when he saw her in the casino. But since the count is now the narrator, Mankiewicz must repeat the end of the casino scene from his point of view and for our clarification. However, the count no sooner enters the plot as co-narrator than he reverts to third person status as Harry takes up the story, describing his meeting with Maria in Rome six weeks later.

The use of an omniscient narrator posed another problem, namely, of explaining how Maria discovered that her husband was impotent. The count told Maria, but she is not one of the narrators. Therefore, Maria will tell Harry in a flashback within a flashback. Except perhaps for *The Locket* (1947), which is a superb example of flashbacks within flashbacks, few films can handle chronological shifts within the past without causing a narrative awkwardness. Had Mankiewicz made Harry the film's sentient center or source of consciousness, the structure would have been less obtrusive. Harry would have had access to Maria's life and could therefore describe everything about it. Clearly what holds the film together is its mythic, not its narrative, underpinnings.

A Film on Filmmaking.   While one would not go quite so far as to call *The Barefoot Contessa* Mankiewicz's *Sunset Boulevard* or even his *Bad and the Beautiful* (although, like Minnelli's film, it opens with a funeral), it does reflect Mankiewicz's ambivalence about the role of mythology in moviemaking. On the one hand, the movies are sustained by their myths. However, those myths must not be the product of the moguls who mold actors and actresses into studio-ordained (or today, media-ordained) types; but by true filmmakers who create myths and mythic figures through language that imparts intelligence and images that bestow beauty. Bette Davis never had better dialogue to speak than she did in *All about Eve*. If her name is synonymous with Margo Channing, it is because Mankiewicz made her look and sound like Margo Channing.

What happens when stars begin to believe their mythology and cannot separate movie reality from objective reality—a confusion that is not limited to stars? Maria gives up her career after only three movies for the "reality" of marriage. When she discovers her marriage can never be real because it cannot be realized, she returns to myth, playing the great mother who attempts to beget the offspring her husband cannot sire. The count seems to want reality: not Maria the movie star, of whose career he is ignorant; but the barefoot dancer he saw in the camp. Yet that dancer was a myth, an avatar of the golden age of innocence to which Maria can no more return than Kane could to the snow-covered farmhouse in the glass paperweight that reminds him of the childhood of which he was robbed. Maria gave up the movies but not their mythology; the count never had the movies but he wants their equivalent. Because Maria wanted reality so badly, she ended up embracing myth; because the count wanted myth, he resorted to reality—murder. But this is what the movies are all about: the reversible conversion of reality into myth. We live life, not myth. When myth becomes a substitute for life, tragedy results; one behaves mythically but acts realistically. A goddess sleeps with men; a maimed nobleman turns to murder. Writer-directors are in the same situation; they have their myths, and they have their words. Images are their link with mythology; language with reality. The fact that neither is sufficient in itself creates a strange dialectic that involves the rejection of myth and language independently of each other and yet the acceptance of myth and language in a union in which each gives up some of its autonomy for the good of art.

Suddenly, Last Summer (1959)

Having portrayed the commoner triumphant, the commoner duped, and the commoner turned contessa, Mankiewicz, in *Suddenly, Last Summer*, offered a portrait of the commoner victimized. Now the aristocrat was not maimed, but mad; and the commoner was not a nightclub dancer but the eyewitness of an event so horrible that her aunt, a New Orleans *grand dame*, wants her lobotomized rather than have her story circulate.

Like the Dunne screenplays, *Suddenly, Last Summer* also showed Mankiewicz's ability to impose his vision on material that was not his. Tennessee Williams wrote the original one-act play that Gore Vidal adapted for the screen.[1] Mankiewicz undoubtedly made his usual contributions, one of which may have been the opening sequence in the operating theater; given his interest in medicine, it is not improbable. But more important, Williams's play presented an extreme version of Mankiewicz's favorite theme. No longer does the aristocrat bait or degrade the commoner; the aristocrat wants to deprive the commoner of humankind's distinctive faculty—reason.

Mankiewicz was also attracted to the play for its theatricality. As a lover of monologues, he probably saw an opportunity to do something with Catherine Holly's final monologue, one of the most spectacular in the modern theater, that would have been impossible on the stage: to dramatize highlights of Sebastian's death as it was being narrated. But before he could do that, he and Vidal had to de-allegorize the plot without letting the narrative collapse.

Suddenly, Last Summer, one of the densest one-acters in the history of drama, is a mosaic of mythic themes: the witch and the maiden; the witch's bribe to the incorruptible hero; the awakening of the sleeping beauty (in this case, with a truth serum); the artist as prey and predator, as Apollo and Dionysus. Williams transmogrifies these motifs. The artist, Sebastian Venable, is a bogus poet who can only write one poem a year that apparently is so bad it must be printed privately. He masquerades as a celibate dressed in white but is really a pederast; he plays the devoted son to his doting mother but uses their blatantly Oedipal relationship as a means of attracting his own kind. When his mother can no longer play the unwitting procuress, he uses his cousin Catherine, dressing her in a white bathing suit that becomes transparent in the water and draws the attention he wants.

As the inverse of the artist, Sebastian inhabits an inverted world; one in which there is no God of love but only of destruction, embodying the violent excesses of nature that Sebastian celebrates in his garden. White/bone/skull is the play's image pattern, with their usual connotations reversed. White is now evil; the skull is not a *memento mori* but the symbol of a vengeful god who strips bones bare. For feeding on the young, Sebastian is fed upon in turn, dying at the place of the skull; on a Golgotha, torn apart in a Dionysian homophagia or flesh-eating ceremony by the boys whom he had corrupted and who have now turned into perverse communicants. Although the Greek law of inexorability operates relentlessly in *Suddenly, Last Summer,* the play lacks the liberating effect of tragedy because there is no tragic protagonist. Yet, besides O'Neill's works, it is one of the few modern American plays that captures the atmosphere of Greek tragedy (Robert Marasco's *Child's Play* [1970] is another) although lacking the cleansing power of its poetry.

Such literary ideas, however, do not fare well on the screen. Vidal and Mankiewicz knew they had to downplay the symbolism which would be difficult since symbol and action were so interconnected. Only once did they fail; since it was a visual failure, one assumes it was Mankiewicz's. At the end, it seemed that Ingmar Bergman took over the direction momentarily; an old lady sitting in a doorway dematerializes into a skeleton; and a statue of the angel of death dominates the hill on which Sebastian is torn apart. But, for the most part, Vidal and Mankiewicz succeeded in making an unusually realistic film out of an intensely symbolic play. They realized that movie audiences must believe, not as myth so much as fact, that something like Sebastian's dismemberment could happen.

The film must not only be realistic; it must look realistic. It was a wise decision to shoot *Suddenly, Last Summer* in black and white; otherwise, there might have been a temptation to reproduce the violent colors of the garden that Williams indicated in his stage directions. Decadence is perfectly possible in monochrome, as Otto Preminger's *Laura* and Albert Lewin's *The Picture of Dorian Gray* (1945) proved. Thus, Oliver Messel created a garden for the film that was quite different from the one Robert Soule designed for the 1958 off-Broadway production. On the stage, the garden was a parody of a Hollywood jungle: Rainbow Island without the soundstage fronds and aquamarine lagoon; evil made lush by the embellishments of nature and forced into a proud acceptance of its symbolism.

In the film, the garden was not so awesomely primeval; Tarzan might have felt at home in it. Since the movie was not limited to the garden set, Mankiewicz did not overwhelm the viewer with the garden's powerful symbolism. He also made the garden more functional. Now it did not compete with Catherine's final monologue; it was the setting in which she delivered it. Mankiewicz also underplayed the decadence so that it did not come in waves, but in touches. Sebastian's study sports a Medusa head on the table, tribal masks on the wall, a court jester's chair, and a print of the martyrdom of St. Sebastian. The eclectic trappings, which were subtly chosen, suit the owner who vacillated between paganism and Christianity, mockery and masochism. Yet one never saw Sebastian Venable, either in the play or in the film. In the play, he was his garden; in the film, he was also his study and his mother, Violet (Katharine Hepburn), who reveled in inversion like her son. Her private elevator was a parody of a Byzantine emperor's throne that would rise during an audience. But, as she explains it, since "we are living in a democracy, I reverse the procedure. I don't rise; I come down." This was a Vidal line, but it could easily have been a Mankiewicz one.

Mankiewicz's artful use of white made Sebastian and Violet alter egos; in fact, their first names, by which they were known socially, recall the twins, Sebastian and Viola, of *Twelfth Night*. Violet appears in white twice, having appropriated her son's color along with its perverted symbolism. But Mankiewicz does not have her wear white in the climactic garden scene. Catherine (Elizabeth Taylor), who has not worn white previously, appears in a lustrous white blouse and black skirt. The moment has come for a confession as stark and unequivocal as her colors.

Since truth is the film's underlying theme, Mankiewicz must establish, at the beginning, the fate that awaits someone like Catherine who dares to speak it. Thus he cannot begin with a shot of the garden which would only accentuate the symbolism he is trying to play down. The opening shot must be of something more realistic: the asylum to which Catherine will be committed if Violet has her way.

The credits appear against a wall. A title gives only the year, 1937. The camera pans the wall, right to left, as it did at the beginning of *Escape*; it stops at a plaque that reads: Lion's View State Asylum. A series of dissolves brings the viewer into the asylum; first into the drum or recreation center where the women stare idly or move in the circular rhythm of madness. The atmosphere recalls the institution in *The Snake Pit* (1948) with which Mankiewicz would have been familiar since he was at Fox when the film was made.

As yet there is no dialogue. A nurse approaches a schizophrenic and leads her out of the drum. The nurse's manner is gentle but firm. The woman's time has come, not to be returned to the dormitory, but to be lobotomized. The next dissolve brings us to the operating theater where Dr. Cukrowicz (Montgomery Clift) is performing a lobotomy. The balcony is packed with students who press so hard against the railing that the bolts loosen.

Here, then, is the main difference between the play and the film. When the curtain rose, the theatergoer saw a garden, every leaf of which was part of an allegory. When the film began, the moviegoer saw a state asylum, every aspect of which was part of the horrifying reality of madness.

With some of the action set in the asylum, Mankiewicz was able to contrast real and imputed madness. Twice, Catherine enters the drum. First, the talk of lobotomy by her greedy mother and brother drives her on to the balcony overlooking the men's recreation center where her presence almost causes a riot. Then, after her confrontation with Violet, she rushes on to the balcony overlooking the women's recreation center and attempts to jump into their midst, thus seeming to substantiate Violet's charge of madness. But it is the inmates who are insane, not Catherine.

These scenes in the asylum are important for another reason. In the play, Catherine had two monologues that followed each other; the first was of her seduction at the Duelling Oaks; the other, the climactic one, on Sebastian's death. Vidal had her tell Dr. Cukrowicz of her seduction early in the film to establish a rapport between them since, eventually, they are to become lovers.

Vidal also had to suggest what Sebastian really was. Williams threw a hint at the end of scene 2 when Catherine spoke of Sebastian's predilection for blue-eyed blonds; but the reference was not especially well motivated. It was the kind of comment one might make in a state of ebbing consciousness or during sleep. Thus, after she nearly precipitated a riot among the male inmates, Dr. Cukrowicz gave her a sedative that, before putting her to sleep, activated memories of that fateful summer when Sebastian's obsession with Teutonic beauty prompted remarks like "This one's eyes are so blue."

Because the plot was so engrossing in itself, Mankiewicz minimized camera movement; there is the usual balance of high and low shots—the latter to suggest dominance. To denote an inverted world, Mankiewicz would sometimes resort to a spatially asymmetric shot in which a character, usually Violet, was at one side of the frame. It is not a film that required much tracking or dollying. With a good script, the camera can simply follow the arcs of thought within the dialogue; panning or tilting, entering or leaving, as the action requires.

Ultimately, it was a tribute to Williams that he could write dialogue with internal movement. In some instances, the sheer grotesquery of the descriptions provided the momentum. But there was also Williams's rhythm that Vidal managed to retain: Williams's slow way of building a scene and structuring the narrative like a fireside tale, retarding the denouement by repetition until the events do not so much reach a climax as explode into one. Mankiewicz also assembled a cast that could give the dialogue the serpentine rhythm needed to make the repetitions seem like clarifications of thought rather than redundancies. Katharine Hepburn's dramatic school delivery gave an air of rhetorical detachment to the story of the sea turtles; and while Elizabeth Taylor's voice was not the subtlest of instruments, the hypnotic quality of the flashbacks made one unaware of her vocal limitations.

The climactic scene must have been enormously difficult to film because Catherine's monologue is interrupted at various points by Cukrowicz, who is functioning as the ideal spectator, asking questions that probably puzzled the audience too. Mankiewicz chose to graft the flashback images—the beaches Sebastian frequented, the white bathing suit he made Catherine wear, his death in the blaze of noon—on to Catherine's monologue. It is as if these images of intense whiteness and heat are burning themselves into her story. Since the monologue is not a conventional one, but rather a disclosure made under the influence of a truth serum, the images must look like suppressed memories that are finally released; they must appear misty, but not blurred or indistinct. To maintain a realistic mood as these images are surfacing from Catherine's consciousness, Cukrowicz's presence must be felt, if only in the form of his off-screen voice. But Catherine's presence must be doubly felt since she is functioning in the dual capacity of patient and participant. It was an unusually complex form, with Catherine and Cukrowicz appearing as narrator and interrogator during the flashbacks, but becoming patient and doctor whenever the action returned to the present.

Psychologically, Mankiewicz has achieved something quite extraordinary: he has dramatized the ego detaching itself from the person and reflecting autonomously. Catherine's face, and sometimes just her mouth, appears in double exposure, as if she were stepping outside

*Katharine Hepburn ascending in her Olympian lift and leaving
sanity below at the end of* Suddenly, Last Summer. *(Credit:
Margaret Herrick Library)*

herself to witness her story. For example, when she describes the beach at Cabeza de Lobo, her face appears in double exposure, right of frame, as the scene materializes. As she relates the incident at the restaurant when Sebastian started to pop pills, the scene fades in behind her; her face again in double exposure, as the hungry children peer through the fence. At the end of the monologue, Mankiewicz cuts sharply from Catherine screaming on the hill at Cabeza de Lobo to her screaming in the Venable garden as she releases the last demon of the past.

It seems almost pointless to debate the veracity of Catherine's account.[2] Williams may have intended the play to end ambiguously, although one doubts that very many theatergoers failed to believe Catherine's story. In the film, one has no reservations at all about her truthfulness.

In the play, Cukrowicz delivered the curtain line with academic restraint, adopting a scholar's qualified tone: "I think we ought at least to consider the possibility that the girl's story could be true." In the film, the line is spoken by Dr. Hockstader (Albert Dekker), a character Vidal added to the plot. Cukrowicz cannot have any doubts in the film because he is in love with Catherine. Hockstader, who wanted the Venable money for the hospital, did have doubts. Now he is the converted skeptic. If anyone is hallucinating at the end of the film, it is Mrs. Venable, who is totally mad and thinks that Cukrowicz is Sebastian. She is last seen sweeping into her Olympian lift and ascending to the heights of sweet delirium. Catherine is still in the garden. "Miss Catherine," Cukrowicz calls. "Miss Catherine's here," she replies. As they leave the garden together, they seem like children awakening from a nightmare into a glorious dawn.

8

The Rialto and the Range

THE NAME of Joseph L. Mankiewicz is not usually associated with the musical or the Western. Although he coauthored the scripts of *Million Dollar Legs* and *Diplomaniacs*, these were comedies interspersed with musical numbers like Paramount's "Road" movies. And although he produced *Three Godfathers* (1936) at MGM, it was not the same as trekking out to the desert for location shooting. However, Mankiewicz has always been partial to anything well written, whether it is a musical comedy libretto or an original screenplay. When Goldwyn hired him to adapt and direct *Guys and Dolls*, Mankiewicz made no substantial changes in the libretto, which had become something of a sacred text, although he deepened the characterizations considerably. In the case of *There Was a Crooked Man*, the screenwriters, David Newman and Robert Benton, presented him with a Mankiewicz-type script, as Philip Dunne had earlier. In each case, the preliminary work had been done before Mankiewicz assumed command.

Guys and Dolls (1955)

Hollywood has managed to film most of the important Broadway musicals, sometimes later than they should have been made—*Carousel* in 1957, *Finian's Rainbow* in 1969; sometimes not as they should have been made—*One Touch of Venus* (1948), *Paint Your Wagon* (1969). Filming started on *Guys and Dolls* four years after its Broadway premiere in November 1950. It may seem odd that *Guys and Dolls* was a Samuel Goldwyn production. Although Goldwyn produced some

Converts and Crooks: (top) Jean Simmons and Marlon Brando, the soul-saver and the high-roller, in Guys and Dolls *(Courtesy Samuel Goldwyn Corporation); bottom, Kirk Douglas and Henry Fonda, the convict and the warden who turns out to be the title character in* There Was a Crooked Man. *(Courtesy Warner Bros.)*

Danny Kaye musicals, he was not a musical comedy specialist like Arthur Freed or Joe Pasternak at MGM. However, like Mankiewicz, Goldwyn was fond of a good story. In fact, he was noted for hiring major literary figures like Lillian Hellman, Sidney Howard, Robert E. Sherwood, Charles MacArthur, and Ben Hecht to write the screenplays for his films. Although Goldwyn made *Oklahoma!* the same year, *Guys and Dolls* was more typical of the producer because it had a stronger book. *Oklahoma!* is often praised for its correlation of music and libretto; but in *Guys and Dolls* it is a matter of integration rather than correlation. Curly's "Oh, What a Beautiful Mornin' " in *Oklahoma!* is just an opening number compared to the kinetic start of *Guys and Dolls* where Broadway's frenetic pace is captured in music and movement, as vendors hawk their wares, hookers swing their purses, and photographers hustle the tourists. This is Gotham, familiar to the locals who see it daily and the folks from the boondocks who have never seen it but know it exists. This is a world of gamblers and their girls, touts, high rollers, and assorted figures of seedy gentility who once thronged the bar at Jack Dempsey's and today can be seen standing at an OTB window, cigarettes dangling from their mouths.

Goldwyn paid one million dollars for the rights to *Guys and Dolls*, outbidding MGM, Columbia, and Paramount. At the time, only two other Broadway plays had commanded such a figure: *Harvey* and *Born Yesterday*, both of which were released in 1950. Although *Guys and Dolls* was budgeted at five million dollars, one would not know it from Oliver Smith's sets. It was not that they looked cheap; they were more surreal and cartoonish than Jo Mielziner's originals. Smith created a New York dreamscape that everyone, the out-of-towners as well as the natives, could recognize as they would figures in a dream—as exaggerated but unmistakable versions of the familiar. Mielziner's sets were more Runyonesque; they had the high-toned flashiness of a milieu where the vernacular had been raised to the level of slick argot and where the amenities meant screwing your opponent without making a mistake in grammar.

The New York of *Guys and Dolls* confirmed the impression that most moviegoers had of the city; an impression that Hollywood perpetuated in scores of films like *Embraceable You* (1948) which opened with an offscreen voice calling New York "a city of tall tales" and a montage of canted shots of skyscrapers suggesting that it was a crazy, lopsided city as well. The New York of *Guys and Dolls* was fabulous in the root sense; it was, as the subtitle indicated, "A Musical Fable of Broadway." The film reproduced this notion of the fabulous metropolis, making no attempt to look realistic. There were no location shots, no rear projection to convey a sense of authenticity. The realism would come from the characterizations. The opening credits showed a neon-lit New York, slightly looney and mildly surreal. It was also a metonymic New York; a New York reproduced in visual shorthand. The letters of familiar names were transposed or the names themselves were abbreviated and sometimes reduced to soundalikes: Trand's (Strand) Bar, Don (Bond) Clothes, Perc's Cola (Pepsi Cola), Sard (Sardi's). This was a New York of metonyms and acronyms, of cropped images, of shifting locations and cockeyed relocations.

In both the musical and the film, the hangout of the guys and dolls was Mindy's—the old Lindy's on 52nd Street and Broadway. In the film, sometimes Mindy's faced Seventh Avenue; at other times, it was located on a side street next to Hav'va Drink, a fruit juice stand like Nedick's. The Save A Soul Mission appeared to be east of Broadway, on 44th or 45th Street; yet it looked out on tenements, scaffolds, and girders—a sight reinforcing the tourist's image of an ever changing New York. Shubert Alley moved up to 46th Street where, above the theaters, perched a washed out billboard advertising a movie with a two-word title: *Best Years*—a Goldwyn self-homage to one of his most honored films, *The Best Years of Our Lives* (1946). But in a musical fable, anything goes; and everything went, especially a sense of place.

Realistic performances were required to counterbalance the stylized production. For this was not a world of square dances but of crap games; the four leads were not a cowboy and his miss, or a carnival barker and his girl, but a gambler and the woman with whom he had been living for fourteen years without benefit of wedlock—Nathan Detroit and Miss Adelaide; and the highest roller of them all and the Broadway missionary who converts him—Sky Masterson and Sarah Brown.

It was especially important to get realistic performances from the four principals, even if it meant casting against type and using nonsinging actors instead of musical comedy types. Cast against type were Marlon Brando as Sky, Jean Simmons as Sarah, and Frank Sinatra as Nathan. Although Sinatra had appeared in musicals at MGM, he would be playing a role that Sam Levene had originated. Vivian Blaine, the original Miss Adelaide, repeated her stage role but never gave it the heart she did in the Broadway production. Blaine never took well to films; she could not adjust her vibrant and essentially theatrical personality to the dimensions of the screen.

When he could, Mankiewicz attempted a quasi-realistic shot, which meant fighting the stylized sets. Sometimes he won, generally in the sense of having activity going on outside that could be seen through the window. But basically, *Guys and Dolls* was antirealistic, with cars moving so slowly on what are supposed to be midtown streets that they seem manned by student drivers. Yet one should not underestimate the performances he obtained from Sinatra, Brando, and Simmons. Sinatra's Nathan was considerably younger than Sam Levene's; hence, Sinatra and Blaine made a more believable couple since Sinatra was only six years older than his co-star as opposed to Levene who was sixteen years her senior. Sinatra was a good-natured Nathan, even willing to mock his own image of the undernourished heart throb by stepping on a scale and weighing in at 125 pounds. Sinatra was also a vulnerable Nathan. When Big Julie forced him to shoot craps with unmarked dice, he was pathetic in his acquiescence. Wisely, Mankiewicz did not insist on an ethnic characterization. Sinatra's Nathan was not Jewish; if he tried to imitate Levene, the results could have been ludicrous. Anyone who saw Levene will remember the helpless shrug he gave in "Sue Me" when he got to the line, "So—nu." In Sinatra's rendition, "So—nu" comes out sounding like "so new." Yet Sinatra delivered the Runyonesque dialogue brilliantly, giving a raffish pedantry to a line like "There are many about whom I would squeal upon with pleasure."

Since he was not a singer, Brando could not invest his numbers with a lyric quality. In this respect, he was like Robert Alda, who originated the role of Sky. Alda's voice had a mellow virility; it was not sonorous or rakish in the tradition of operetta. Brando's had a streetwise smokiness. The sound was slightly foggy, a bit raspy, but perfect for "Luck Be a Lady" which could easily become an aria in the hands of a self-enraptured baritone.

"Luck Be a Lady" is sung in the film, as it was in the play, during the crap game that Nathan is forced to hold in the sewer because no other place is available. Like Mielziner's set, Smith's was playfully surreal, with just a few authentic touches (coils, tunnels, ladders, drainage pipes) to suggest a sewer but one that has taken on the colorful attributes of the gamblers. The sewer itself is a witty blend of constructivism and surrealism, with the objects being readily discernible but rendered in colors that ordinarily are not associated with them. Although one can identify the object, it has also lost its status as object, becoming an artifact of the surreal. The ladder is bright red; the cables are a multicolored band. The cement floor becomes polished hardwood, ideal for ballet; a lamp hangs from the ceiling as it might in a back room during a dice game. Wearing a black suit, a tie with a dice motif, and a broad-brimmed Fedora, Brando sings "Luck Be a Lady" as if he were making a sexual threat, intimidating Dame Fortune by pointing a finger at her before she points one at him.

Of all the characters in *Guys and Dolls,* Sarah Brown profited most from Mankiewicz's realistic approach. Since she obviously interested Mankiewicz more than the others, he altered the characterization so there would be nothing about her to suggest an ingenue. He saw her as a woman dedicated to an apostolate, but expending passion on it that would be better lavished on a lover. Rather than resort to dimestore psychology and portray her as repressed, Mankiewicz chose a different route: he had her straightjacketed by her uniform. Unconsciously, she feels emotionally suffocated by it; thus she never buttons her jacket completely. The kindly Brother Arvid is always buttoning her up as if it were a daily routine. When Sky invites her to dinner, she automatically reaches for the errant button. During "I'll Know," she plays with it. When Sky notices the loose button, she says apologetically, "It's a nervous habit."

But it is a habit Sarah has no great desire to break; if anything, she would prefer to be totally unbuttoned. Mankiewicz wrote new dialogue for the Havana sequence to accentuate Sarah's dormant femininity which awakens after a few Dulche de Leches which she thinks are milkshakes. At first, the third button is not in line with the others. After a few drinks, her jacket is completely open and her inhibitions have vanished. Simmons does not overdo the tipsy bit. Sarah may be a virgin, but she is not committed to that state. "Tell me how to live," she asks Sky. As a missionary, she wants to give him help—"truly personal help." Her offer of help was really an offer of herself. "I've got to know what you're thinking," Sarah insists. "I'm thinking you better have your dinner," Sky answers as he buttons her up.

Years of circumventing the Production Code taught Mankiewicz the art of writing coded dialogue. But the dialogue in the Havana sequence was not double entendre; it caught the undercurrent of longing in a lonely woman's words. By giving that dialogue a kinesthetic dimension, Simmons created a woman with a sense of mission but with needs that religion alone could not satisfy.

The film retained most of the original score, but, as usual, there were casualties and additions. Purists complain because one of Frank Loesser's best duets, "I've Never Been in Love Before," sung by Sky and Sarah after their return from Havana, was replaced by "A Woman in Love." While it may lack the rapture of the original first-act duet, "A Woman in Love" is less operatic and more suited to the vocal abilities of Brando and Simmons. While Brando could handle "Luck Be a Lady" and Simmons did nicely by "If I Were a Bell," neither could do justice to "I've Never Been in Love Before." "A Woman in Love" is also one of those musical comedy rarities: a song whose lyrics fit the mood, the action, and the character. First it is heard softly on a guitar when Sarah is playing tourist; it picks up a mambo beat in the nightclub; finally, it becomes Sky's hymn to Sarah's transformation.

"A Bushel and a Peck," a jukebox favorite, was dropped in favor of the pedestrian "Pet Me, Poppa." Sky's ode to New York at dawn, "My Time of Day," was omitted, although the music was heard when Sky and Sarah walked toward the mission at daybreak. In the original, Adelaide and Sarah met once, at the end, when they joined voices in a duet, "Marry the Man Today," which seemed to be the only reason for bringing them on stage together. The duet was contrapuntally interesting but not a major loss; nor was Arvid's sentimental "More I Cannot Wish You" which sounded like "Too-Ra-Loo-Ra-Loo-Ra."

Mankiewicz effected a rather subtle change at the end. The movie seems to conclude as the musical did; it does, but with a twist. At the end of the stage version, Sky and Sarah have already married, and Sky is now a member of the mission band. Nathan is running a newsstand and is finally about to marry Adelaide. Still thinking in crap game terms, he has trouble finding a "place" for the wedding. Finally, Arvid offers to marry them at the mission.

Perhaps influenced by Shakespeare's way of uniting couples in double (*A Midsummer Night's Dream*) and quadruple (*As You Like It*) ceremonies, Mankiewicz chose a joint tying of the knot for a more climactic effect. The doors of Mindy's open, and two waiters exit with twin wedding cakes. The procession attracts some onlookers who follow the waiters as they proceed to Duffy Square. The gamblers begin the wedding march, followed by the chorines from the Hot Box. Mindy's truck pulls up, depositing the two grooms. Lieutenant Brannigan arrives, now friend rather than foe, and gives Adelaide away; Arvid does the same for Sarah. It is the wedding of the year, judging from the crowds that press against the couples. As they drive off, the bustle of the opening scene is repeated. Suddenly the guys and dolls freeze into a still—a crazy snapshot a tourist might send home as proof of having seen Baghdad on the Hudson.

There Was a Crooked Man (1970)

The credits split the screen, and in so doing, become a metaphor for the film which itself is split; it is part Western, part prison drama with the distinction as thin as the line that divides the murals on the left of the frame from the credits on the right. At the beginning, one does not know it will evolve into a prison drama; images of a masked rider on horseback keep dissolving into each other as an offscreen voice sings the title song, one of those jaunty ballads that has to be scored with a twang, as if the entire orchestra had become one big "gee-tar." Like the prefigurative credits, the lyrics do not lie:

> There was a crooked man,
> He rode a crooked mile;

He always wore a crooked smile.
Of all the crooked men
In the crooked west,
He was the crookedest.

There will be a crooked man in the literal and figurative sense. But who—the robber, Paris (Kirk Douglas) or the warden, Lopeman (Henry Fonda)? Certainly not Abe Lincoln–Tom Joad–Mister Roberts Fonda. But wait.

Mankiewicz was attracted to the Newman–Benton screenplay for several reasons. First, it would be a challenge to make a prison Western. Mankiewicz's only experience in either genre was *Manhattan Melodrama* which he coauthored and *Three Godfathers* which he produced. There was also the script's revisionist approach to the West of the 1880s. In the Old West, no one ever seemed to urinate; in the New West, they do. But above all, the script maintained a fine line between cynicism and misanthropy. *Crooked Man* is cynicism leavened not by wit but by a Juvenalian rhetoric that a satirist uses when wit is out of place, as it would be in a prison break Western. This kind of rhetoric can take several forms, with a certain overlapping: parody, indignation, and antithesis (the tradition-bound past versus the traditionless present). In *Crooked Man* Mankiewicz is making an implicit pact with the audience, saying, in effect: "You've seen Westerns and prison films, and so have I. But I've made neither. Although my last two films were flops, my eye is not jaundiced, only badly bloodshot. So here goes."

The opening shot of horses' hooves wrapped in burlap to cut down on noise signals the kind of film it will be. A house is going to be robbed; but houses have been robbed in scores of films, and such precautions were never taken. Inside, a black domestic wearily ties her bandanna into a knot, sighs resignedly, and just as she is about to enter the dining room, affects a Mammy's satisfied "Mmmmmmmmmm" and proceeds to serve a family she loathes. As the father begins a hypocritical grace, the camera tracks back, revealing the table surrounded by gunmen. Their leader is neither a masked desperado nor a giggling psychopath; he is Kirk Douglas flashing a smile so radiant one does not know if it is the luster of integrity or the glitter of guile.

Crooked Man took advantage of the liberalized Production Code that came into existence in 1968 (it was Mankiewicz's first and thus far only R-rated movie) while, at the same time, parodying the period that saw such drastic changes in movie morality. Mankiewicz showed bare breasts; a judge in a bordello drooling over the bosom of a prostitute who bites her nails in boredom; males nude from the rear, including Kirk Douglas hitching his gunbelt around his waist; conversations during urination; flies being buttoned up; and a head forced down the seat of an outhouse. When Paris escapes, it is a trail of horse dung that leads Lopeman to him.

Yet the film was also a sendup of the 1960s when anyone who wore rimless glasses was an activist; and anyone who preached prison reform and looked like Henry Fonda was incorruptible. Paris wears rimless glasses, but they pick up an inordinate amount of glare. The reason, we discover at the end, is that the lenses are window glass. Better to see you with, my dear. Similarly, Lopeman with his Lincolnesque bearing and silvered sable beard is—you guessed it—the title character.

The well plotted screenplay left nothing to chance. If the film is a prison Western, Paris and Lopeman must be outlaw and sheriff as well as convict and warden. To effect a plausible transition from one role to another, the script first showed Lopeman as a sheriff who prided himself on being able to apprehend a criminal without a gun. Unfortunately, he tried his liberal charm on someone who shot him in the leg, thereby making him the crooked man of the title. His failure as a sheriff is responsible for his becoming the warden of a desert stockade where Paris is serving his sentence for robbery.

Once the action moves inside the stockade, the film takes on the conventions of the prison drama; or rather its plot conventions since Mankiewicz makes even less of an attempt to emulate the style of the prison drama than he did of the Western. However, the screenwriters and Mankiewicz (who made his usual changes in the script)[1] had seen enough prison films—*Brute Force* (1947), for one—to supply the necessary motifs. The criminals, who make the great escape at the end, must be a diversified lot, as indeed they are: a youth who killed a man with a billiard ball; the petty thief who shot Lopeman, and a duo that Paris calls the "daisies"—Cyrus and Dudley, who have fallen into the roles of uxorious husband and nagging wife. True to form, there is a homosexual guard with eyes only for the young Coy, but he is nothing like the neo-Nazi Hume Cronyn (who plays Dudley) created in *Brute Force*, which also seems to have provided the motif of the sacred picture—the lady of the prison cell. In *Brute Force* the prisoners recalled their women by gazing at a picture of a woman on a calendar. In *Crooked Man* the prisoners force Dudley to draw breasts on the angel he has sketched on the wall so that they can have something resembling a female.

While the Dudley–Cyrus relationship exists in prison films (although it is more common in a women's prison movie like *Caged*), it is more characteristic of the Western where men are often forced into male/female roles. In *Red River* (1948) Walter Brennan functions as a kind of wife-cook to John Wayne; when Wayne finds a surrogate son in Montgomery Clift, Brennan shifts his affection to an Indian, assuming the dominant or masculine role and treating the Indian like a squaw.

Inevitably, there will be a clash between the warden and the convict, but what precipitates it is a moral issue with political implications. Lopeman wants to run the prison as if it were a socialist collective with the prisoners working together to build their own mess hall. Yet it is an impossible goal because Lopeman is a conservative at heart and susceptible to corruption. The film makes a connection between Lopeman's politics and his morals. He is appalled by prostitutes and naked women, in the flesh as well as in pictures. His is the kind of virtue that easily turns to vice because it is disguised self-righteousness. Paris is genially amoral and will sacrifice anyone to escape from the stockade. Paris can tolerate the crudities of prison life because at least they are not pretentious; but he cannot tolerate home cooking for prisoners as a means of impressing the local politicians. Thus, he precipitates a riot on the day of the dedication of the mess hall.

While the prisoners fling their dinners at the dignitaries, Lopeman remains impassive, bearing the humiliation like a martyr. His apathy is a mockery of social action; it is tolerance reduced to the absurd; to turning not the other cheek but the entire face. He is as blind as the painting of Blind Justice under which he sits.

Like any art, cinema can work on an associative level, encouraging us to draw on our knowledge of movie history and place the film we are seeing in its genre and within the context of the performers' screen careers. To see Henry Fonda as a phony liberal is to witness the transmogrification of the Fonda image. Lopeman is Tom Joad turned fascist; Mister Roberts as Captain Queeg; Abe Lincoln as Franco. Although Fonda went the villainous route in *Once Upon a Time in the West* (1969) the year before, he did not purport to be anything other than a villain; or, as Roy Rogers would say, a varmint. In *Crooked Man*, he is Janus-faced; at the end, he choses one profile over the other.

Douglas at least began his career as a heel in *The Strange Love of Martha Ivers* and created one of the screen's smarmiest opportunists in *The Big Carnival* (1951). Although *Carnival* was a newspaper melodrama about an anything-for-a-scoop reporter, the screenwriters forged a subtle link between Douglas's earlier film and *Crooked Man*. In *Carnival* Douglas, en route to cover a rattlesnake hunt, explains his theory of journalism to a cub reporter with an appropriate analogy. If fifty rattlesnakes were loose in a city, to sustain interest and sell papers the reporter would make sure that the snakes were rounded up gradually, until all but one has been accounted for. Just as interest is about to wane, the last is caught, having been concealed all the time in the reporter's desk drawer.

Crooked Man, which begins on a note of cynicism as a black servant makes herself into Aunt Jemima, ends with the incorruptible lawman succumbing to the charms of corruption, but at the expense of Paris, who dreamed of an Eden but forgot that its first resident was a serpent. After the breakout, Paris returns to the rattlesnake nest where he has hidden the $500,000 in a saddlebag and a pair of bloomers. Shooting the snakes, he retrieves the money. But as he is untying the bloomers, a snake leaps out, biting him in the neck. "Oh, shit!" he whines—fitting last words for a film that used the real thing as well as the expletive. Lopeman finds the body and, slinging it over a horse, returns it to the stockade. But he does not accompany the body. Slowly, he rollᶜ a cigarette—something he could never do before. The bogus liberal has become a true capitalist. At the moment Lopeman crosses the Mexican border with the $500,000, the film swings full circle as the title song is heard not in English but in Spanish; and the end title, "And he lived happily ever after," thumbs its nose at those who believed the gospel according to *The Shadow*: crime does pay, and quite handsomely.

There Was a Crooked Man followed *The Honey Pot*. While neither was a success, *Crooked Man* came closer to being a true movie. Although Newman and Benton were in a borrowing vein when they wrote the script, they borrowed from other films, not from literature. Robert Benton, in fact, is still borrowing; now a screenwriter-director like Mankiewicz (*Bad Company*, 1972; *The Late Show*, 1977; *Kramer vs. Kramer*, 1979), he confused homage with appropriation in *Still of the Night* (1982) in which he paid tribute to Hitchcock by incorporating plot details from his films. The motifs in *Crooked Man* may have been unoriginal; even the rattlesnake death came from another movie, *Lust for Gold* (1949). The film, however, is not unoriginal because the motifs appear in a new setting: the West as seen through eyes that resisted the myopia of the 1960s but could not recover their lost innocence.

Mankiewicz brought out the sardonic quality of the script, although one could easily see the film's becoming a dark allegory under someone else's direction. But Mankiewicz knew it was an extended joke cast as a ballad with a punch line for a denouement. He did little visually, yet one wonders if anyone, except a combination John Ford–Jules Dassin, could really envision a prison break Western. Mankiewicz managed a few Fordian touches. The long shots had the look of framed vistas; entrances and openings served as means of masking the frame. The entrance to the stockade provided a natural mask; a shot through a hole blasted in the refectory wall recalled the shot from the cave mouth in Ford's *The Searchers* (1956). However, Mankiewicz was too dependent on the zoom, using it when a tracking shot would have been preferable; as it would have been when Coy was about to be flogged. Instead, the camera zoomed out, flattening the image.

On the other hand, prison life does not lend itself to gorgeous color. Rather than attempt anything expressionistic with bars and shadows *à la* Fritz Lang's *You Only Live Once* (1937), Mankiewicz stayed within the parodistic perimeters of the script. But he was still biding his time. The right property had not yet come along; and until it did, he preferred parody to prostitution.

9

The Eagle and the Asp

Julius Caesar (1953)

OF ALL THE works Mankiewicz adapted for the screen, Shakespeare's *Julius Caesar* was the indisputable classic. This is not the same as saying it is his best adaptation; far from it. Whether a work that has achieved greatness in its own medium can achieve it in another is problematical. Filmed Shakespeare is a case in itself mainly because of the amount of scholarship a filmmaker must absorb before deciding on what approach to take to the text. Olivier's *Henry V* (1944) drew the viewer into the Elizabethan soul; his *Hamlet* (1948) into the recesses of the collective unconscious. *Julius Caesar,* however, is not a play that adapts well to the screen despite Dore Schary's eccentric claim that it is "the most cinematic of all of Shakespeare's plays." There is no real poetry in *Julius Caesar*; only rhetoric which, while it can be powerful on the stage, can seem ponderous on the screen. In film, rhetoric often translates into weightiness which is difficult to criticize without seeming to be anti-intellectual. Mankiewicz made a noble attempt to film *Julius Caesar,* but it clearly was not his favorite Shakespearean play (is it anyone's?). When one realizes that his burning ambition was to make the movie version of *Twelfth Night,* it is amazing that he was able to direct a respectable, if not deeply felt, *Julius Caesar.*

Mankiewicz made *Julius Caesar* at MGM shortly after he left Fox at the end of 1951. It was one thing for Irving Thalberg to produce *Romeo and Juliet* at MGM in 1936 when movies were a mass medium. It was something else for MGM to film *Julius Caesar* in 1952 when Dore Schary was head of production and television was the mass medium. There is a great disparity between the austerity look of *Julius Caesar* and

"O pardon me, thou bleeding piece of earth," Antony (Marlon Brando) begs of the dead Caesar in Julius Caesar. *(Credit: Margaret Herrick Library)*

the fanfare that accompanied its premiere at one of New York's legitimate theaters, the Booth. John Houseman, the film's producer, need not have feared that *Julius Caesar* would be "swamped by production";[1] Schary saw to it that it was not. One of the unsolved mysteries of movie history is how *Julius Caesar* won an Oscar for art direction–set direction (black and white).

When MGM filmed a classic, it often reminded the audience it would be watching something of literary significance by putting the credits on a scroll, on the pages of a leatherbound book, or against a heraldic or iconographic background that bespoke seriousness. *Julius Caesar* opens in this way, with the credits moving up the screen against an image of the Roman eagle as Miklós Rózsa's tense chords slowly relax into the lyric tenderness of the Brutus theme. A printed prologue, an excerpt from Plutarch's life of Caesar, states, in effect, that Caesar's becoming dictator for life made him "odious to moderate men." It was not North's translation, but the prose had a pristine quality. Then, another title appears: Rome 44 B.C. Although the amount of print was not excessive by either Hollywood's or Mankiewicz's standards, the gravity of the introduction tended to reduce the viewer to a student.

Julius Caesar is only occasionally cinematic. Although it is difficult to open up a play of this sort, it should have been possible to suggest a broader canvas, a less circumscribed world. But, for the most part, everything seemed cabined and confined; except for the assassination and the funeral oration, there were few surprises. One expected the opening scene to be dominated by the garlanded bust of Caesar, as it was; one also expected Flavius to undeck the bust, as he must. But one did not expect the Roman citizens to look like the toga-clad extras of *The Sign of the Cross* (1932) and *The Last Days of Pompeii* (1935), but they did.

When Orson Welles filmed *Macbeth* (1948) at Republic, it did not look like a Poverty Row production. Yet much of *Julius Caesar* looks like the aftermath of a budget cut. This time MGM did not live up to its "Art for Art's Sake" motto. The mechanical thunder and lightning that flash over the forum on the eve of Caesar's assassination would not even alarm the pusillanimous. Worse were the moundlike buff on which Cassius commits suicide against a soundstage sky; Caesar's ghost in an ectoplasmic double exposure that even the horror unit at Universal would have found tacky; and the tents at Philippi, more medieval than Roman, that appear to have been left over from the joust scenes in *Ivanhoe* (1952).

At least the battle of Philippi was not soundstage; it was filmed at Bronson Canyon near Hollywood Boulevard. Yet it looked like an ambush in a B Western. The forces of Antony and Octavian were marshaled on a hill; those of Brutus and Cassius proceeded along the plain below.

At a given signal, arrows flew, javelins were hurled, and the cavalry charged down the hill. It was as if that familiar sentence from first-year Latin had suddenly come to life: "Falling upon the enemy, the Romans slew them."

Generally, what one gets in *Julius Caesar* are Mankiewicz's insights into the play, as if he were a professor sharing his ideas with students in a seminar. The soothsayer should be blind, tapping his way with his staff. His reaching out to touch Brutus's face, and then recoiling after warning Caesar to beware the ides of March, was a splendid touch. So were some of Mankiewicz's attempts to keep the action from settling into weightiness—a difficult chore when a filmmaker could not add to the text but only subtract from it.

To extract some drama from Caesar's speech about Calpurnia's nightmare (act 2, scene 2), Mankiewicz had Calpurnia utter the actual words that Caesar said he heard her speak in her sleep: "Help, ho! They murder Caesar." Mankiewicz was also successful in supplying a visual context for one of the most familiar lines in the play: Caesar's observation, "Yon Cassius has a lean and hungry look" (act 1, scene 2). In the film, Caesar noticed Cassius signaling to Casca; and what seemed to be an offhand remark in the play became a reaction to a disturbing incident.

These were mere touches; in the two crucial scenes, Caesar's assassination and Antony's funeral oration, Mankiewicz did more than supply embellishments; he delivered the goods. Since Caesar's death was a ritual slaying of the tyrant who is sacrificed for the good of the state, Mankiewicz imparted a ritualistic quality to the assassination. He alternated high and low angle shots of the conspirators at Caesar's feet as they petitioned for Publius Cimber. When Caesar, photographed at a low angle, looked down on them, the effect was a striking juxtaposition of power soon to be lost and impotence about to turn to revenge. Mankiewicz starts the assassination in long shot as Casca walks from the back of the senate chamber to strike the first blow; then he cuts to a subjective tracking shot of a figure staggering toward Brutus, following it with a shot of the figure itself—the bloodied Caesar clinging to Brutus and expiring with the famous, "*Et tu, Brutè*? Then fall Caesar" (act 3, scene 1). Originating in long shot, the assassination concludes in long shot—with the assassins washing their hands in Caesar's blood.

Mankiewicz did not regard the assassination of Caesar and the rise of Antony as separate events but as interrelated parts of a whole. Therefore, he connected them visually by beginning each with the same kind of formalized long shot. The assassination started with Casca's walking into the frame from the rear of the senate chamber. Afterward, Antony walks the length of the corridor and into the frame, traversing what seems to be an enormous distance.

As one might expect, Antony delivers his oration on the steps of the capitol. Mankiewicz, who has a strong archetypal sense, uses steps ambivalently throughout the film as a symbol of the ascent to power and of the fall from eminence, having made a similar association between stairs and dominion in *House of Strangers.* At the Lupercalia, Cassius follows Brutus up the steps, gradually winning him over to the conspiracy with arguments that became more persuasive as they kept ascending. When Artemidorus attempted to give Caesar the letter warning him of the conspiracy, he stands midway on the steps which seem endless, discouraging any intervention in the affairs of destiny.

Like the assassination, the funeral oration sequence begins in long shot, with Antony at the top of the steps as Brutus descends to address the mob—his authority diminishing by degree. At one point, Brutus appears overwhelmed by the populace that seems to rise up like an engulfing wave. Mankiewicz cuts from Brutus on the steps to the mob below, as he does again when Antony occupies the steps for his oration. Mankiewicz, who has a stage director's instinct for making the setting part of the drama, uses the steps of the capitol as Eisenstein had used the steps of Odessa in *Potemkin* (1925), charging them with associations of power and bloodshed. When Antony descends the steps with Caesar's body which he places on the landing, one thinks of *Potemkin* and the mother standing on the landing with the child in her arms; the Cossacks at the top, pointing their guns at her, and the trail of bodies below.

Mankiewicz also converts the steps into a courtroom so that they become the setting for the forensic drama which Antony generates. After haranguing the mob, Antony proceeds horizontally across the steps, parallel to the landing where Caesar's body lies, the parallel movement denoting his alliance with Caesar's cause. When he cries, "Here is himself, marred as you see with traitors" (act 3, scene 2), he pulls the sheet from the corpse. Mankiewicz must suggest that, during these courtroom theatrics, Antony is manipulating his jury. Thus when Antony pauses, it is not to weep despite his admission of a heavy heart; it is to revitalize his passion, as Mankiewicz makes clear when he cuts to a shot of Antony's eyes that look like coals defying the embers to form.

Mankiewicz was able to make effective cinema out of these two sequences because they possessed the kind of drama that could be converted into film. Rhetoric, of which there is a preponderance in the play, can turn into heaviness with the wrong cast. For some of the roles, Mankiewicz inherited MGM's grand bourgeoisie. Since Calpurnia and Portia were not starring roles, they should not have been played by leading ladies. As Calpurnia, Greer Garson looks like Mrs. Miniver in curls; as Portia, Deborah Kerr, with her cascading hair and billowing nightgown, exudes a sensuousness that would have been more appropriate for Juliet on her wedding night. Louis Calhern's Caesar resembles the chairman of some board; Calhern conveys Caesar's pomposity but none of his weakness despite the fact that Shakespeare portrayed him as a partially deaf epileptic and a coward in the water.[2] Few tragic figures have been saddled with so many defects. But *Julius Caesar* is a play about defective human nature: "The fault, dear Brutus, is not in our stars, / but in ourselves" (act 1, scene 2). Brutus's alleged idealism, extolled by academics, is political naiveté. He votes against killing Antony, refuses to involve Cicero in the conspiracy, and holds a gentleman's view of assassination: "Let's kill him boldly, but not wrathfully" (act 2, scene 1). His greatest mistake, which makes him a textbook case of hamartia, is allowing Antony to speak at the funeral.

For Brutus, Cassius, and Antony, Mankiewicz was not limited to the MGM regulars; he was fortunate since these were the roles that, if miscast, would make the film as tedious as a bad debate. As Brutus, James Mason is the perfect embodiment of the cerebral revolutionary. By maintaining an anguished sensitivity throughout the film, Mason proves Mankiewicz's thesis that Brutus is the true hero of the play. Thus his death could not be a conventional suicide but rather a romantic envoi; Mankiewicz has him embrace Strato as he falls on the sword. By contrast, Cassius dies ingloriously, forced to prevail upon a hulk of a soldier to dispatch him.

John Gielgud's Cassius lies somewhere between Richard III and a Restoration fop whose hair falls in effete ringlets. Gielgud creates a Cassius of contradictions, resolving them by his interpretation so that they seem to be balanced opposites. Thus Cassius can be bookish but curiously anti-intellectual; a dispassionate conspirator but a sentimental friend who bids a tender "forever, and forever, farewell" to Brutus.

Given Brando's tendency to slur syllables and mumble, his Antony is unusually articulate. Antony must look athletic, for as the play begins, he is about to run at the Lupercalia. Brando tends to project a masculinity that is introspective and threatening—a quality that Mankiewicz catches in the opening scene as Antony steps forth, bare-chested and glistening, when Caesar asks him to touch the infertile Calpurnia during the race.

Yet Antony proves hardly incorruptible. His funeral oration is rabble-rousing, but at least Mankiewicz gives him a rabble to rouse. In fact, the mob is so unruly that Antony's plea, "lend me your ears," for once makes sense. This Antony is as power-hungry as Caesar; when he begs the "bleeding piece of earth" to pardon him, he is sincere, for he sees himself in the dead dictator. After the assassination, he contemplates the bust of Caesar, turning it around to face him.

When one realizes how self-seeking Antony has been, his calling Brutus "the noblest Roman of them all" at the end of the play may seem ironic. Yet Antony is sincere. By "noble," he does not mean magnanimous or royal. He means that Brutus's motives far surpassed those of the other conspirators because, essentially, they were selfless. In view of the nobility that informed Mason's Brutus, Mankiewicz wanted Antony's tribute to be taken literally. Thus he gave the last scene a ritualistic grandeur by fading out on Brutus's corpse which, of course, meant the elimination of Octavius's closing speech—hardly a loss.

Throughout *Julius Caesar*, one has the feeling that Mankiewicz had a vision of the ancient world that he was unable to express because his primary responsibility was to Shakespeare's text. It is frustrating to a filmmaker to be able only to delete—to purge the text of puns, anachronisms, and repetitions; to cut the descriptions of the battle of Philippi which would be shown, however inadequately—but not to be able to add. In *Cleopatra*, Mankiewicz was able to offer the portrait of antiquity that fidelity to Shakespeare prevented his realizing in *Julius Caesar*.

Cleopatra (1963)

Cleopatra was so overpublicized and, for the most part, so unfairly reviewed, that one would never guess it was one of the more historically accurate films about the classical world. Since the history of *Cleopatra* has been sufficiently documented, a summary of the facts must suffice.[3] As in the case of *A Letter to Three Wives*, Mankiewicz was not the original choice for director but was hired at the end of January 1961 after Rouben Mamoulian resigned; and an evolving script of several hands, including those of Nigel Balchin, Lawrence Durrell, and Dale Wasserman, proved unfilmable. On 13 October 1962 Mankiewicz showed Zanuck a rough cut that ran four and a half hours. When Mankiewicz did not edit the film to Zanuck's satisfaction, Zanuck fired him ten days later. Within two months, there was a businesslike reconciliation between the men, and Mankiewicz went to Spain to refilm the battle of Pharsalus which had been hastily shot in the summer of 1960. When *Cleopatra* opened in New York on 11 June 1963 the running time was 243 minutes; by 17 June it had been reduced to 222 minutes.

The credits attribute the screenplay to Mankiewicz, Ranald MacDougall, and Sidney Buchman. When Mankiewicz claimed sole writing credit, the arbitration committee of the Screen Writers Guild ruled that he would share credit with Buchman, who had written an outline, and MacDougall, whom Walter Wanger hired to write a rough draft based on Buchman's outline. While the dispute is common knowledge, what is not generally known is the fact that, in the Fox archives, there is a memo (9 November 1961) by Molly Mandaville, Zanuck's assistant, comparing MacDougall's 226-page second draft screenplay (completed 23 August

1961) with Mankiewicz's incomplete 178-page shooting script of 18 September.

According to the memo, Mankiewicz made dialogue changes in almost every scene, dropping some sequences and adding others in addition to making alterations in content and tone. He expanded Cleopatra's triumphant arrival in Rome, the most spectacular scene in the film, from MacDougall's mere five and a half pages to thirteen and a half. He dropped the Nile sequence as well as Caesar's wedding to Cleopatra which had been covered in the dialogue. What particularly impressed Mandaville, in addition to Mankiewicz's improved characterizations of Caesar, Antony, and Cleopatra, was the intelligence that guided his changes. MacDougall had Caesar demand, at a banquet, that the senate crown him emperor—a setting that Mandaville believed "detracted from the seriousness of the demand." Mankiewicz switched the scene to Cleopatra's villa.

In MacDougall's draft, Antony no sooner returned from Caesar's funeral than he was making love to Cleopatra, admitting that he even loved her when Caesar was alive. "This scene," Mandaville argued, "holds little promise for their future relationship because the audience won't care what happens to them." Mankiewicz ended the first part of the film with a strong Antony, whose degeneration in the second part made for greater contrast. If Antony were an impetuous lover, Cleopatra would never have considered him as a replacement for Caesar in her plan for a world empire. Mandaville concluded her comparison by noting that "these changes were not accomplished by someone using a blue pencil"; the changes took "time and thought."

And art, one should add—an art that was apparent at the very beginning when the credits appeared on a pink mural flecked with gray, anticipating the soft pinks and blues that predominate in the film and giving the illusion of a world veiled, but not obscured, by time. First to be seen on the mural are the faces of Cleopatra, Antony, and Caesar—their features inspired by the leads: Elizabeth Taylor, Richard Burton, and Rex Harrison. As the credits continue, the images become historical; the last credit coincides with the final image which freezes into a stop-frame—or what Mankiewicz in his script calls a "frieze-frame" (a stop-frame resembling an image on a frieze)—of the opening scene: the battle of Pharsalus. The frame is then activated, springing to life as the battle concludes and an off screen voice delivers the prologue in the classical style:

And so it fell out that, at Pharsalia, the great might and manhood of Rome met in bloody civil war. And Caesar's legions destroyed those of the great Pompey, so that now only Caesar stood at the head of Rome. But there was no joy for Caesar, as in his other triumphs. For the dead which his legions counted and buried and burned were their own countrymen.

Thinking perhaps in terms of *All about Eve*'s five-act structure, Mankiewicz fashioned the final screenplay in five acts, each beginning with a "frieze-frame" that is activated after a voice-over introduction; and, except for act 4, each ending with the frieze image that would introduce the next act.

Act 1, Pharsalus (48 B.C.), begins with a frieze-frame of the battlefield, with voice-over narration explaining that the conflict between Caesar and Pompey led to civil war. The act ends with an eagle on a Roman banner dissolving to a frieze eagle.

In act 2, Alexandria, Rome (48–47 B.C.), the frieze eagle becomes an eagle on the ship bringing Caesar to Alexandria. There follows a voice-over comparison of the Roman civil war with the power struggle in Egypt between Cleopatra and her brother Ptolemy: "And even as Caesar's galleys sailed the great sea to Egypt, it was happening that, just as the Romans, so the Egyptians, made war one upon the other. For young King Ptolemy would no longer share the throne with his sister Cleopatra, and he drove her from the city of Alexandria and sought to destroy her." The act ends with a long shot of a Roman galley followed by a frieze-dissolve to the Roman forum.

Act 3, Rome (46–44 B.C.), begins with a frieze-frame of the Roman forum with a voice-over introduction explaining Caesar's absence from Rome: "But only after more than two years and many wars in Africa and Asia Minor, was Caesar able to cross over to Italy and come home at last to celebrate his triumphs." The act ends with Cleopatra's sailing for Egypt after Caesar's assassination, with a fade-out for intermission.

Act 4, Philippi, Tarsus, Rome, Alexandria (42–31 B.C.), opens with a fade-in on the frieze of Philippi with the narrator's voice summarizing events between Caesar's assassination in 44 B.C. and Philippi in 42: "And for more than two years did Antony strive against the assassins of Caesar. At last, at Philippi, in Macedonia, he was able to meet them in battle. Cassius was the first to die, by his own hand. Then Brutus and the others." The act ends with Octavian hurling a spear at Cleopatra's tutor, Sosigenes, with a frieze-dissolve to Cleopatra's palanquin at Actium.

In act 5, Actium, Alexandria (31–30 B.C.), the palanquin is brought forward after a voice-over narration explans the significance of Actium: "And so once more, the Romans warred upon each other. And just as Antony had foretold, the forces of Octavian came to meet them on the spot where they landed, which was at Actium, in Greece." The act ends with the narrator's voice repeating the dialogue between Agrippa and Charmian as the camera tracks back from Cleopatra's body on the catafalque to Agrippa standing at the entrance—the final frieze.

The structure of *Cleopatra* was the culmination of techniques that Mankiewicz had used earlier. The frieze-dissolves harked back to the stop-action shots of *The Philadelphia Story* and *All about Eve* and the dissolves of *The Barefoot Contessa* and *Suddenly, Last Summer;* the division into acts was anticipated by the segmented narrative of flashback films like *A Letter to Three Wives* and *All about Eve*. The flashback dissolves of *Suddenly, Last Summer* inspired the assassination scene in *Cleopatra*. On the ides of March, Cleopatra consults a medium. As Cleopatra looks into the burning coals, she sees, as if through a cloud of smoke, the assassination taking place. Superimposed over images of the assassination is Cleopatra's face, as Catherine's was over the flashback montage in *Suddenly, Last Summer*. In each film, Taylor's face seemed to bleed into the frame, becoming one with the events portrayed.

While other writers may have contributed to the script of *Cleopatra*, the overall design was Mankiewicz's; and, one suspects, most of the dialogue. It is difficult to imagine anyone other than Mankiewicz having Caesar say to Cleopatra, "Have you broken out of your nursery to come here and irritate the adults?"; having Antony tell Octavian, "It is possible, Octavian, that when you die, you will die without ever having been alive"; or giving Cleopatra such a wonderful put-down when Antony admits his fondness for "almost all Greek things": "As an almost-all-Greek thing, I'm flattered."

However, dialogue is only a vehicle for characterization, and it was in the characters of Caesar, Cleopatra, and Antony that Mankiewicz rewrote the authorized Hollywood version of ancient history. In *Julius Caesar*, he was saddled with Shakespeare's incomplete Caesar portrait along with Louis Calhern, who did not even fill out what was there. In *Cleopatra*, Mankiewicz could draw on the classical sources as well as on the talents of Rex Harrison, who comes closer to the historical Caesar than any other actor is ever likely to. Unfortunately, moviegoers know Caesar, if at all, as a composite of Douglas MacArthur and Benito Mussolini; or, if they took second-year Latin, as the author of the *Gallic War* with its famous opening sentence, "All Gaul is divided into three parts." What most moviegoers do not know is that Caesar was a man of letters as well as a great general. His commentaries on the Gallic and civil wars, which are excellent journalistic prose, are among the better examples of the Attic style in Roman literature. In the film, Caesar has a scribe at his side on the plain of Pharsalus. "Let what I have said be set down," he commands. Like a historian, Mankiewicz is suggesting that, just as Alexander included epic poets in his entourage, Caesar may well have traveled with an amanuensis to whom he dictated material for his commentaries.

Caesar. The average moviegoer probably did not know that Caesar was also a wit, whose collected sayings (*Dicta Collectanea*) have been highly admired. However, Mankiewicz knew it; hence, the casting of Harrison was thoroughly consonant with what was known of the historical Caesar. Mankiewicz also knew how to integrate an actor's screen persona with his character. Today, a moviegoer would associate "et cetera" with Yul Brynner in *The King and I* (1956). But in 1963, there were many moviegoers who would have seen the original film and the original king: Harrison in *Anna and the King of Siam* (1946). To them, "et cetera" evoked the name of Rex Harrison as well as Yul Brynner. In *Cleopatra,* when the chief eunuch Pothinus introduces Ptolemy with all of his honorifics, Caesar interrupts with a list of his own titles and then adds, "et cetera, et cetera."

There was a human side to Caesar that Mankiewicz never fails to disclose. Despite his desire to be emperor (although one doubts that he would ever have taken the odious title of *rex*), Caesar was uncommonly magnanimous. He pardoned the poet Catullus for composing lampoons about him. Catullus was primarily a love poet, but he occasionally engaged in political satire. In poem 93, which is just an epigram, Catullus laughingly claimed he did not care if Caesar were black or white. In the film, Mankiewicz has Caesar quote the poem.

Caesar also pardoned Brutus for siding with Pompey in the Civil War. Mankiewicz could not give the complete background of the Civil War, and cuts in the film prevented his using the motif of Pompey's ring as comprehensively as he had planned. Julia, Caesar's daughter and Pompey's wife, gave her husband a ring which the Egyptians returned to Caesar after they killed Pompey. Caesar was to pass the ring on to Caesarion, his son by Cleopatra. After Caesarion's murder, the ring was to fall into Octavian's possession. Mankiewicz obviously had in mind Wagner's *The Ring of the Nibelungs* in which the ring, as it changed hands, brought misfortune to the owner. Although the handing down of the ring now stops with Caesar, one can see how Mankiewicz was trying to dramatize the shifting of power through the symbolism of the ring. But what is significant is the fact that Caesar accepts the ring from the Egyptians and wears it around his neck. Clearly he felt something for his former son-in-law for whom he ordered a ritual burial.

Even with a layman's knowledge of antiquity, one could sense that Mankiewicz assimilated his sources and knew how to work his research into the dialogue without seeming to toss in learned allusions as fringe benefits for the classically educated. He embedded the allusions in the action, so that they were dramatically and visually natural. During the Moon Gate battle, when Caesar cried, "The turtle!" the soldiers raise their shields over their heads in a battle formation known as the *testudo* or "turtle." Caesar's obsession with having a son prompts Cleopatra to remark that, according to popular opinion, Brutus is his illegitimate son, a point that Plutarch makes as well. Antony's warning to Cicero that the orator's tongue will lead to his decapitation, and Cicero's reply that the instrument will more likely be Antony's sword, reflects exactly what happened the year after Caesar's death.

Historians have always been puzzled by Antony's behavior at Actium. Cleopatra, believing he had been killed, turned her barge back to Alexandria. When Antony saw what was happening, he deserted his men and pursued her. Robert Payne, who found *Cleopatra* historically accurate except for the fact that Actium was a skirmish rather than a full-scale battle, has conjectured that Antony was drunk, which would fit the picture of Antony the inebriate that Cicero painted in the *Second Philippic*.[4] Interestingly, Mankiewicz had Antony at the stern during the battle, brandishing a wine cup.

Mankiewicz either dramatizes history or draws inferences from it. One of his inferences, and a sound one, is that Caesar's desire to be emperor or sovereign ruler may have been fed by Cleopatra who, not understanding the political machinery of the Roman republic, kept reminding him: "Kings are not elected. Gods are not elected."

Cleopatra.   When a historical allusion backfires, it is not Mankiewicz's fault but the performer's. While Elizabeth Taylor could project the dynastic passion that passes for love among monarchs and could trade insults like a sparring partner, she was at a loss when she had to speak dialogue with classical names. When she must say, "Did you know that Apollodorus would kill Pothinus?" one had the impression she did not know who each was, although the former was her major-domo; and the latter, the chief eunuch. Equally embarrassing was her literary conversation with Caesar in which she noted that his writing was "different" with "perhaps too much description."

When Taylor was not forced to talk "literary criticism" or do map-reading, she was quite believable. Perhaps because she was groomed from childhood to take her place among Hollywood, and then international, royalty, she conveyed the feeling that, to Cleopatra, passion, power, and dominion were often identical. Throughout the film, one is watching a woman whose ambitions are sparked by an erotic energy that even infuses the language with which she describes her grand design—the fusion of Rome and Egypt into a world empire, jointly ruled by herself and Caesar; or, when his death intervened, by herself and Antony. Although Caesar was the means of insuring the grand design, she did love him. What she felt for Antony was an amalgam of love, hate, pity, and finally the infinite understanding that the dying have for the dead. Thus Cleopatra's passion is grander than sexual attraction; it is the assimilation of the erotic into the larger context of empire; an assimilation that is sexual primarily in the sense that an empire requires a dynasty to sustain it.

The grand design did not preclude human feelings. In their scenes together, Harrison and Taylor expressed the mutual attraction that must have existed between Caesar and Cleopatra, both of whom knew the loneliness of power and the exhausting feeling of unreality that came from being a symbol. When they are alone, they are people as well as monarchs. Caesar can admit his fear of having an epileptic seizure in public; and when he has an attack in Cleopatra's presence, she ministers to him compassionately.

When Cleopatra bears Caesar a son, Caesarion, he welcomes her to Rome in a ceremony celebrating the procreative power of the woman who called herself the Nile. Trumpets sound a fanfare; bowmen shoot arrows into the air; and a pyramid splits open, releasing a flock of birds. Dancers in zebra-striped bras and G-strings with leopard tails undulate and writhe. Finally, Cleopatra enters the forum through the arch, riding on a gigantic sphinx of black granite, dragged by slaves. When the sphinx is within sight of Caesar, the throne on which Cleopatra and Caesarion are sitting is detached, carried down the steps, and placed in front of him. The spectacle is at the juncture of splendor and decadence where it belongs. Nominally, Rome was still a republic; the Age of Nero was still more than a century away.

Antony.   With Caesar's assassination, the film reverses itself. The second half duplicates the first, both visually, with a dissolve from Alexandria to Rome; and dramatically, with Cleopatra's futile attempt to give Antony a sense of imperial destiny and make him her colleague in the grand design. However, Antony lacks a ruler's soul; only the excesses of court life appeal to him. While Cleopatra had been on an equal footing with Caesar, she is forced to become Antony's superior because she realizes the extent of his weakness. Thus she must demand obeisance and even marriage from him.

Since Taylor and Burton were committing the most widely publicized adultery in Hollywood history while they were making *Cleopatra*, they brought to their roles all the tension, passion, and anxiety they were experiencing in real life. When one realizes that each was married at the time, there is something uncannily accurate about the way Cleopatra reacts to Antony's marriage to Octavia: she wrecks his room in a scene that is too uncomfortably close to reality to qualify as mere acting.

With Caesar, there was the possibility of a world empire; he could respect the monarch and the woman in Cleopatra. Antony cannot respect the monarch because he does not understand monarchy. With him, Cleopatra drops her royal defenses and becomes pure woman. For them, there is no grand design; only what Shakespeare in *Antony and*

Cleopatra (act 3, scene 13) called a "gaudy night." With Antony, Cleopatra has become more of a passionate lover than a passionate queen. When she comes to Tarsus she receives Antony on her royal barge, making her appearance from behind a curtain as if she were a madam and the world her bordello. Knowing his penchant for bacchanals, she stages one that parodies their own relationship. A satyr and a Cleopatra lookalike grope each other as girls in grape-clustered outfits perform a mock ballet that ends with Antony's embracing one of the dancers on a revolving couch. Caesar's tempering influence has vanished.

Mankiewicz will give Cleopatra a tragic grandeur at the end, but, in the meantime, he must dramatize an affair in which the participants are too self-willed to compromise and too caught up in the coils of passion to extricate themselves. What keeps Cleopatra from being just another *grande amoureuse* is a quality she shares with other great rulers: an awareness of her place in history that allows her to practice a fatalism that otherwise might be construed as blind acceptance. Mankiewicz gave Cleopatra a sense of historical awareness that Taylor converted into an amoral fatalism which worked, but not on the lofty level that Mankiewicz had envisioned.

With Antony there is not even fatalism; only dissipation. After the defeat at Actium, he retires to the tomb of the pharoahs to nurse his wounds, becoming the embodiment of tragic waste without the tragic flaw to redeem it. Yet, at this moment, Antony is wonderfully human; there is no hamartia to cover his situation. In a gratuitous action that would have appealed to André Gide, Antony charges into the midst of Octavian's army, striking at the soldiers' shields with a mere sword. But none of the soldiers retaliates; Antony is too pathetic to kill. One thinks of Ajax slaughtering a flock of sheep or of King Lear crying "Blow, winds, and crack your cheeks" (act 3, scene 2).

Tragic Diction. At the end, Mankiewicz elevated *Cleopatra* to as high a tragic level as he could. He succeeded because he understood movies and moviegoers. He did not give them Shakespeare; he did that in 1953. Instead, he gave them imitation Shakespeare; not classical tragedy but the popular equivalent, something like Northrop Frye's low mimetic in which the characters were like ourselves. Mankiewicz's Antony and Cleopatra were like ourselves in their emotions but not in the way they expressed them. They did not speak in the vernacular but in the low mimetic or the low tragic. Their dialogue had the cadences of classicism without sounding quaint or archaic. Mankiewicz's language is strong on rhetoric; sentences often fall into equal parts with counterbalancing rhythms. Demanding obeisance from Antony, Cleopatra says, "I asked it of Julius Caesar; I demand it of you." It is also language in which one puts

down a rival by repeating his word order. When Germanicus mocks
Octavian's claim to be Caesar's heir, he says derisively, "Antony, stay not
too long in Alexandria," which Octavian tops with, "Germanicus, stay
not too long in Rome."

There is also the unmistakable aura of poetry in the final scenes when
Antony and Cleopatra speak as doomed lovers. Although Mankiewicz
did not write the dialogue in verse, he achieved the effect of verse by
avoiding normal word order and using a rhythm based on the succession
of images rather than ideas. Catullus's poetry was to have played a much
larger role in the film than it finally did. A blind bard was to have recited
the famous "Let us live and love" (poem 5); and Antony was to have
expired with a Catullan lyric on his lips. Mankiewicz works the substance of poem 5, in which Catullus asks Lesbia for an infinity of kisses to
ward off unending night (that is, death), into Antony's final speech: "You
and I—we will prove death so much less than love. You and I—we will
make of dying nothing more than one last embrace. A kiss. To take my
breath away."

Burton gives Antony's dialogue an eloquence that is neither stagy nor
declamatory. When Cleopatra compares him to Caesar, he replies with a
tirade in which he keeps repeating Caesar's name the way Shylock keeps
repeating "bond" in *The Merchant of Venice* (act 3, scene 3). In his death
scene, Burton's voice has the dying fall the dialogue required.

Elizabeth Taylor and Richard Burton as the immortal lovers in
Cleopatra. *(Credit: Margaret Herrick Library)*

To set Antony and Cleopatra alongside other tragic lovers, Mankiewicz interwove elements of Shakespearean tragedy into the conclusion. First there is the motif of the wrong inference that owes something to Romeo's committing suicide because he believes Juliet was dead. In the film, when Apollodorus tells Antony that Cleopatra is waiting for him in "the last possible place," Antony assumes he means that she has killed herself; consequently, he does the same. When Antony is hoisted up the wall into the mausoleum where Cleopatra and her handmaidens have retired, one almost expects Cleopatra to cry, "Welcome, welcome!" as Shakespeare's heroine did. Just before Antony dies, he asks for a kiss, like Othello. When he expires, a *Hamlet*-like silence prevails: "There has never been such a silence," Cleopatra says, astonished. Before she reaches into the basket of figs for the fatal asp, she experiences immortal longings and dresses in gold. Shakespeare's Cleopatra feels she is becoming pure spirit; Mankiewicz's Cleopatra experiences a Platonic reverie: "How strangely awake I feel. As if living had been just a long dream—someone else's dream—now finished at last. And that now will begin—a dream of my own which will never end." To rephrase Wordsworth, our death is but a sleep and a forgetting.

When Agrippa enters the tomb, he finds Cleopatra lying in state in a golden robe and her handmaidens pressing against the catafalque. An asp slithering across the floor makes it clear that they have emulated the queen's death. Shocked, Agrippa asks the dying Charmian, "Was this well done of your lady?" To which Charmian replies, "Extremely well done, as befitting the last of so many noble rulers." The exchange is a paraphrase of *Antony and Cleopatra* (act 5, scene 5):

> FIRST GUARD: What work is here, Charmian? Is this well done?
> CHARMIAN: It is well done, and fitting for a princess
> Descended of so many royal kings.

The camera then tracks past Agrippa through the doors of the mausoleum that function as a natural frame, expressing the point of view of the spectator standing at the entrance. For this is what one has been throughout the film: a spectator of the past watching antiquity being animated like frescoes brought to life. The frame then freezes for the last time; the colors fade; and the final image becomes part of the mural of history.

Cleopatra was the companion film to *Julius Caesar.* In the intervening decade Mankiewicz had the opportunity to rethink *Julius Caesar,* or at least as much of it as he could incorporate into *Cleopatra.* True to tradition, the conspirators plot amid thunder and lightning; the eve of the assassination is marked by prodigies and Calpurnia's dream of Caesar's statue spouting blood. There is even a visual reference to the earlier film. The leaves swirling across the patio of Cleopatra's villa recall those that blew across the forum in *Julius Caesar*. Mankiewicz chose not to compete with himself by redoing the two most memorable sequences in *Julius Caesar*—the assassination and the funeral oration. In *Cleopatra*, both were completely visual; there was no dialogue since no one would ever be able to improve upon the language Shakespeare wrote for the two most dramatic episodes in the play. Thus, the assassination was done through a series of optical dissoves; and there is no funeral oration, only the burning of Caesar's body on a funeral pyre in long shot.

Perhaps the greatest similarity between the two films is Mankiewicz's visual homage to Brutus and Cleopatra. Both films end with the characters' bodies ceremoniously displayed. Brutus may have been the noblest Roman of them all, but Cleopatra's nobility extended beyond the Tiber.

10

The Celluloid Stage

MANKIEWICZ'S outstanding gift, and at the same time his chief source of frustration, has been his ability to express life in terms of theater. Theoretically, this talent should have led him to Broadway which, for him, will always remain the road not taken; although to his admirers, he made the right choice in the yellow wood. It may be flattering to be known as the Philip Barry of the screen, especially if one's idol is Barry; but the title is a blessing and a curse. It is like being reduced to an identification in a matching test: Joseph L. Mankiewicz = filmic theater, just as Edgar G. Ulmer = PRC and Max Ophuls = dolly shots. The phrase, "filmic" or "filmed theater" *(le théatre filmé)*, suggests a movie whose sequences are acts and whose curtains are fade-outs. However, *le théâtre filmé* does not adequately define what Mankiewicz does, even though he does use the equivalent of act division and curtain lines. What emerges in a Mankiewicz film is not an action staged proscenium style but one enclosed within a different type of frame—celluloid frames which, when projected, acquire a mode of existence known only to the movies.

Although *All about Eve* portrays life in the theater, it does so in a way that is cinematic. The film has become a major part of movie mythology; the lines have been quoted so often, especially by Bette Davis mimics of both sexes (is there any female impersonator who has not said, "Fasten your seatbelts. It's going to be a bumpy night"?); and Margo Channing is such a familiar name in the movies' registry, that we forget that *All about Eve* was intended for the screen and could not be duplicated in any other form, as the Broadway musical version *Applause* (1970) showed, without a corresponding loss of art.

Like *A Letter to Three Wives*, *All about Eve* originated as a *Cosmopolitan* short story, Mary Orr's "The Wisdom of Eve" (1946), in which the stage-struck Eve Harrington charmed herself into the good graces of

Bette Davis as the legendary Margo Channing in All About Eve. *(Credit: Margaret Herrick Library)*

Broadway star Margola Cranston, whom she used as a means of further-ing her own career. However, all moviegoers are not readers of *Cos-mopolitan.* To reach an audience that included the sophisticates who have strolled through Shubert Alley and the theater novices who think it is a passageway lined with garbage cans, Mankiewicz had to make the characters universally recognizable types. Addison De Witt (George Sanders), the drama critic, was Mankiewicz's own creation; he appeared in neither Mary Orr's story nor in *Applause,* which was a conflation of Mankiewicz's script and Orr's story. Addison is also absent from the dramatization that Orr and her husband, Reginald Denham, did of the story which is also called *The Wisdom of Eve* (1964).

Although modeled after George Jean Nathan, who made poinards of sentences, Addison was sufficiently effete, barb-tongued, and dandified to evoke what audiences in the hinterlands would consider a Broadway swell. The aging star must be a star and bear the name of a star. Bette Davis was not the original choice for Margo Channing, Mankiewicz's improvement over the original name. The director originally wanted Claudette Colbert, probably because she conformed to what most moviegoers imagined a Broadway star to be. Yet Davis's mythology was so powerful that it made no difference what kind of star she was, Broadway or Hollywood; Bette Davis was star. Everyone knows an Eve Harrington (Anne Baxter): the quiet worker who gets promoted over her peers whom she then fires and replaces with her own staff; the "I'll do anything for an A" student who not only will but does. Then there were the theater types: Max Fabian (Gregory Ratoff), the ulcer-ridden producer; Lloyd and Karen Richards (Hugh Marlowe and Celeste Holm), the talented but gullible playwright and his sincere but easily duped wife; Bill Sampson (Gary Merrill), the tough-talking director; and last, but never least, Margo's wisecracking but gold-hearted maid, Birdie (Thelma Ritter). One has seen them everywhere, but not at their best; for that, one must look to the theater.

But this is the theater as portrayed by a man, who, although he has chosen to live in the East, at the time was still guided by the conventions of the "life in the theater" movie which was different from the kind of film Hollywood made about itself. However, "guided" was all Man-kiewicz was.

Hollywood versus Broadway

Films about attaining stardom in Hollywood never portrayed it as an easy undertaking, but there was usually someone around to help the newcomer get started. In *Variety Girl* (1947), the only reason for having Paramount's leading stars cooperate to give Mary Thatcher her big break was to demonstrate Hollywood's magnanimity. *A Star Is Born* (1937) was similarly self-congratulatory, arguing that, at least in the movies, there was always a Norman Maine who was willing to take the big swim for a Vicki Lester. Hollywood implied that such altruism was rare on Broadway. In the movies, one might have to sleep with a producer to get a role, as Kim Stanley did in *The Goddess* (1958); but in the theater one might have to kill him, as Rosalind Russell did in *The Velvet Touch* (1948). Theater people generally were self-enraptured, like Katharine Hepburn in *Morning Glory* (1933) and Coral Browne in *Auntie Mame* (1958). Ambition unsexes the stage actress (Hepburn) while it makes the movie star a love goddess (Stanley). A Broadway producer who plays the tyrant ends up friendless (Robert Montgomery in *The Saxon Charm*, 1948); a Hollywood producer can treat his colleagues shamelessly, but they are still willing to work for him (Kirk Douglas in *The Bad and the Beautiful*). And when a Hollywood producer dies he receives a Viking funeral, buried at sea in an actual blaze of glory (Richard Mulligan in *S.O.B.*, 1981).

Movie people tend to be sentimental, hovering around the silent star when she returns to her old studio (Gloria Swanson in *Sunset Boulevard*, 1950). It is the movie star, not the stage actor, who gets the bravura mad scene. When a stage actor goes bonkers and thinks he is Othello (Ronald Colman in *A Double Life*, 1948), there is no staircase to descend as there was for Swanson in *Sunset Boulevard*; no Erich von Stroheim standing alongside the cameras to guide the distracted star.

Mankiewicz very cleverly framed the soundstage within the proscenium in *All about Eve*, intermingling the conventions of the Broadway and Hollywood film so that the characters were neither pure stage nor movie types but composites of both. The theater people are cool but concerned; clever but dupable. The aspirant is talented but needs a *deus ex machina*. Even Miss Caswell (Marilyn Monroe), who is supposedly angling for a career on the stage, seems more like a Hollywood starlet on the threshold of fame, as Monroe was at the time. What made *All about Eve* such a popular success, as distinguished from most movies about the theater (for example, *The Velvet Touch; The Saxon Charm; Main Street to Broadway*, 1953; *Forever Female*, 1953, which failed to attract mass audiences), was Mankiewicz's ability to play to the second balcony as well as to the front orchestra.

All about Eve may well have been about Broadway; Alfred Newman's spirited prelude and postlude made audiences feel they were at a play. Yet *All about Eve* had the soul of a movie, with familiar character types and even more familiar techniques. The form was one that audiences knew: flashbacks within a frame narrative. Mankiewicz used the framing device of the Sarah Siddons awards dinner, freezing the action into a still when the aged actor (Walter Hampden), in medium long shot, presents Eve with the gold statuette; then Mankiewicz segues into a five-part flashback as Karen, Margo, and Addison spend the evening remembering Eve, the "golden girl"; finally, Mankiewicz unfreezes the frame as Eve accepts the award and allows the film to proceed to its conclusion.

All about Eve (1950)

Unlike many flashback films, All about Eve was carefully planned. No narrative is unmediated; the story is being told by someone—an "I," a third party, an omniscient narrator, a narrator-agent. Although Mankiewicz appeared to be using three narrators, he made one of them, Addison De Witt, the supreme consciousness; a surrogate director to whom he delegated authority. While Addison is given a flashback of his own, one which he must introduce because he is the only witness to the event, he has also been entrusted with the introductions. Mankiewicz has him nod in Karen's direction when he finishes introducing the main characters, as if to give her the cue for the first flashback.

The structure of All about Eve anticipated Cleopatra's with its five-act division. However, as a flashback film, Eve also contains a prologue and an epilogue: prologue: the Sarah Siddons awards dinner; Addison in voice-over narration introduces characters; freeze; Addison turns over narration to Karen; act 1 (Karen): Eve approaches Karen at stage door; Karen introduces Eve to Margo, who takes pity on her, making her secretary-confidante; act 2 (Margo): Margo covers the time from Bill's departure for Hollywood to his disastrous homecoming-birthday party when she realizes Eve has taken over her personality as well as her lover; act 3 (Karen): Karen relates the way she detained Margo so Eve could go on in her place; Addison's voice intrudes to deliver a capsule review of Eve's performance ("superb"); act 4 (Karen): Eve blackmails Karen to get role in Lloyd's new play; act 5 (Addison): Addison describes New Haven tryout where he unmasks Eve; dissolve of Eve's face to floral piece on banquet table as frame unfreezes and Eve accepts award; epilogue: Eve returns to her apartment to discover a fan waiting for her—Phoebe, who will be her parasite as she was Margo's.

Although Eve's form, like that of many screenplays, is derived from the drama, the expression of that form is peculiar to film. The opening image denotes the kind of movie Eve will be. The first shot is of the gold statuette with an inscription—"The Sarah Siddons Award for Distinguished Achievement in the Theatre: Miss Eve Harrington"—that Addison's voice-over narration proceeds to explain. At the outset, there is an alliance of word, voice, and image—the key elements of the narrative.

Because Mankiewicz keeps the action moving, especially during moments of pure dialogue, *Eve* never succumbs to stasis or verbosity. The camera moves when it should, and Mankiewicz cuts when he must. As soon as Addison's voice identifies the "distinguished looking speaker" as the aged actor, the camera tracks back, showing the actor as well as the others who have gathered for the occasion, until the entire room is framed in an extreme long shot. Mankiewicz also found the cinematic equivalent for building to the first appearance of the main character. Mankiewicz uses twelve cuts (for example, of Lloyd, Bill, Addison, the award) before he shows Margo; and even then, she appears metonymically—as a hand reaching for a cigarette. Finally, in the thirteenth shot, Margo appears in close-up with the ubiquitous cigarette.

Eve must tell her story to Margo and the others in the form of a monologue, but it cannot be a stage monologue photographed in one unbroken shot like Ingrid Bergman's in *Under Capricorn* (1949). She is telling a story that must convince cynics like Margo and Birdie. The tale touches on so many themes—a childhood of fantasies, her first exposure to little theater, a wartime marriage, her husband's death, her hand-to-mouth existence—that there is something to which everyone can respond. Thus Mankiewicz cuts on reaction; yet he makes the reactions part of the monologue so that one is never conscious of its being interrupted. Eve's description of her childhood strikes a responsive chord in Margo, to whom Mankiewicz cuts at the moment she extinguishes her cigarette and starts listening in earnest. When Eve remarks that the unreal was always what was real to her and then chides herself for talking gibberish, Mankiewicz cuts to Lloyd as he springs to her defense; since he is a playwright, he understands that the theater is the art of making the unreal real. As an ex-vaudevillian, Birdie would sympathize with someone in financial straits; hence the cut to her is appropriate when Eve explains how her husband's insurance money enabled her to stay in San Francisco.

Just as there was a cinematic form behind *Eve*'s theatrical structure, there was a human drama beneath the film's brittle veneer. Mankiewicz found the same vulnerability in Bette Davis that Edmund Goulding discovered earlier in *That Certain Woman* (1937) and especially in *Dark Victory* (1939). But what was a luminous vulnerability had darkened with age. To paraphrase one of Davis's best-known creations, Fanny Skeffington, a woman is never more defenseless than when she is middle-aged and about to be eclipsed by a rival. But the rival was not the conventional villainess. Eve is the other side of Addison. In fact, one thinks of them as a pair; Addison and Eve, the first parents of the theater. Eve may be duplicitous; and Addison, merciless. Yet, paradoxically, they are necessary to insure the perpetuity of the stage—Addison by his

"*Addison and Eve*": *Star and Critic engulf a starlet—Bette Davis, Marilyn Monroe, and George Sanders in* All About Eve. (*Credit: Movie Star News*)

religious commitment to it that drives him to demand perfection of all who work in the theater; Eve by making her ambition the base of the blue flame of her talent.

The dedication and passion the theater requires can be sexually enervating. Addison is not hetero-, homo-, or even asexual; he is metasexual. His desire to possess Eve is like Waldo's desire to possess Laura in the film of that name—as an art object, not as a woman. Eve is feminine only when she is manipulating a man; otherwise, she looks androgynous.

In a scene that some have found mildly lesbian, a girl in Eve's boardinghouse, perhaps her roommate, phones Lloyd, telling him worriedly that Eve is ill and hinting that he should come over, which he does. One has no reason to doubt the girl's sincerity until the camera pulls back, revealing a smiling Eve. Arm in arm, she and the girl walk up the stairs like an old married couple. Eve has rewarded her lackey with an embrace—or perhaps more. But the point is that Eve can offer anyone whatever kind of affection is needed at the moment; and a moment is all it will last.

At the end, the film comes full circle, with Phoebe's insinuating herself into Eve's graces as Eve had into Margo's. Phoebe has even acquired Eve's androgynous look, now that she is playing handmaiden to Eve's Wonder Woman. Phoebe did not exist in the original Orr story. Mankiewicz created her, perhaps in reply to *Stage Door* (1937) which also came full circle as another Terry Randall arrived at the Footlights Club to become another link in a chain that originated with Thespis and stretches out into infinity. However, the Terry Randalls of the theater were decent human beings; Phoebe comes from a different race.

It is interesting that Mankiewicz calls Eve's successor Phoebe, an early moon goddess and another name for Artemis (Diana), the goddess of the hunt. Phoebe, then, is a predatory moon goddess; as such, she conforms to the image most moviegoers would have of a teenager hell bent on a career in the theater: a lunar creature, cold and intimidating, as opposed to the solar deities who make it in Hollywood. The ladies of the moon are as incandescently white as the lights that spell out their names on marquees. Significantly, the final shot—one that is completely without dialogue in a film that is prized for its dialogue—is one of dazzling brightness. Holding Eve's statuette, Phoebe bows in front of a three-mirrored cheval that multiples her image, so that one sees a myriad of Phoebes bowing to each other—a race without end, because its originator is the mother of us all: Eve.

Sleuth (1972)

In *Eve*, the theater was a metaphor for life; in *Sleuth*, theater *is* life. In *Eve*, although theater was all, all was not theater. Margo was finally able to separate the woman from the star, a distinction Eve will probably never be able to make. In *Sleuth*, Andrew Wyke (Sir Laurence Olivier), a writer of detective fiction, is so far removed from objective reality that the line of demarcation between life and pretense has vanished, along with the distinctions between on and offstage, the boards and the prop room. In *Sleuth*, Mankiewicz has reduced theater to game—in itself, not the highest form of theater. But when a game is played well, with wit and ingenuity, when the contestants speak dialogue instead of clashing wordlessly, and when that game grows into a plot—then it can be consummate theater, especially if the plot involves one of the oldest subjects in literature—adultery.

Knowing that Milo Tindle (Michael Caine) has been sleeping with his wife, Marguerite, Andrew invites him to his Dorset estate, Cloak Manor, and makes him a nonrefusable proposition. He asks Milo to stage a robbery that will leave Marguerite bereft of her jewels, Milo in possession of Marguerite, and Andrew ensconced with his Finnish mistress whom he vastly prefers to his wife. What Milo does not know is that Andrew's game involves the degradation of the player. After tricking

Milo into dressing up as a clown and ransacking the house, Andrew shoots him. On the stage, this was the first-act curtain. Since there was another act, one assumed that when the curtain went up, Milo would not be dead—at least not yet, although he would be at the play's conclusion; but not until he has subjected his host to a humiliating charade of his own.

Anthony Shaffer's 1970 play, one of the most successful thrillers in stage history, was a study of game in all its aspects—social, sexual, and aesthetic. In the play, Andrew lauds the games-player as "the complete man . . . of potent passions and bright fancies," a fairly accurate description of himself as well. Fancy rules Andrew's life, enabling him to be director, scene designer, playwright, and protagonist in life's theater—a point that the credits themselves make. The credits appear against a stage; not the world stage of *Cleopatra* but a miniature one that might be used for a puppet show. Zooms reveal a series of macabre sketches, illustrations from Andrew's novels. The last sketch is of Cloak Manor which freeze-dissolves, like the frescoes in *Cleopatra,* into the house itself. And just as Alfred Newman's overture to *Eve* anticipated a rising curtain, John Addison's neoclassical prelude to *Sleuth* with its macabre harpsichord motif creates the same expectation.

In *Eve,* onstage and backstage were distinct. Margo had to remind Eve that the wardrobe mistress, not the actor, picked up the costumes once the performance was over. But in *Sleuth,* where everything is theater, everything is either a prop or a part of the set, and that includes Cloak Manor.

The grounds of the manor are dominated by a maze of hedges with protruding gargoyles. The hedges themselves are in sections, so they can swing open like gates. Within the maze, near a liquor cabinet in the shape of a sarcophagus, Andrew sits, dictating his latest novel into a tape recorder and speaking in the voices of his characters. The interior of Cloak Manor is no less theatrical. The cellar is part dungeon, part storeroom with a stage trunk overflowing with costumes. The living room is filled with automata that are set into motion by the push of a button or the pull of a switch. There is Jack Tar, the jolly sailor with the uncontrollably raucous laugh; the bewigged lady who pounds away at the harpsichord; and a ballerina who does mechanical pirouettes. Even Marguerite's portrait (which is actually one of Joanne Woodward) is a participant in the drama, as Gino's was in *House of Strangers.* Mankiewicz will cut from the automata, who look alive even when they are not moving, to a close-up of the portrait, so that everything in the room becomes a spectator. At the end, when Andrew kills Milo, the automata spring into mechanical life, blindly executing their movements like an audience that has been conditioned to respond to a bloody ending.

The automata are the supporting cast as well as the audience for the games Andrew and Milo play. Andrew and Milo are the only humans in the cast. Although *Sleuth* was a two-character play and a two-character movie, Schaffer, who adapted his play, tried to dispel that impression; otherwise it would ruin the game. As playwright, he made the playbill part of the game; as screenwriter, he did the same with the opening credits. The playbill included three other "characters"—Inspector Doppler, Detective Sergeant Tarrant, and Police Constable Higgs. Doppler was the disguise Milo assumed when he returned to subject Andrew to the same treatment he had received, after having told Tarrant what had transpired earlier at the manor. Higgs was supposed to arrive with Tarrant at the end of the play.

As a film, *Sleuth* gave the impression of an even bigger cast. In addition to Doppler, Tarrant, and Higgs, there was also Teya, Andrew's mistress, played by the fictitious Karen Minfort-Jones; and Marguerite, played by one Eve Channing—clearly a Mankiewicz touch. Originally, the production notes listed the name of the actress as Margo Channing, noting that this, of course, was not her real name but that the performer (one Jean Emily Trimmier) adopted it as her stage name after seeing *All about Eve*. Eve Channing was a better ruse; Margo's name, which ranks with Rick Blaine, Vicki Lester, and Scarlett O'Hara, was too well known.

Masters of the game: Michael Caine and Sir Laurence Olivier in Sleuth. *(Credit: Margaret Herrick Library)*

Although the film version follows the play fairly closely, it eliminates the more theoretical discussions of games, and emphasizes the type of game a movie audience would understand—the game of discrimination whose rules are simple: the superior exploits the inferior. Accordingly, Shaffer changed Milo from a travel agent to a hairdresser; from part Jewish to Roman Catholic; and from a Tindle to a Tindolini, which his Genoese father shortened to Tindle so the family could "become English." However, Milo, who is not in the least embarrassed about his origins, has named his hairdressing salons, Casa Tindolini. Thus the confrontation between Andrew and Milo is not the usual one between the cuckolded husband and the lover, but between a native Englishman and an immigrant's son whom Andrew, in one of his less euphemistic moments, calls a "wop."

The screenplay's orientation is in perfect accord with a theme that Mankiewicz had been exploring ever since he became a filmmaker. However, he found the portrayal of one male's victimizing another more challenging. The drama had a homosexual aura that could be faint or pronounced depending on how Andrew was played and how the actor playing him delivered the speech in which he asked Milo to forget Marguerite and live with him: "You and I are evenly matched. We know what it is to play a game."

In the screenplay, Schaffer did not minimize the suggestion of homosexuality. However, the casting of two unmistakably heterosexual actors in the roles created something quite different—an atmosphere of frustrated homosexuality. Andrew is practically impotent. Consequently, virility infuriates him, causing him to inveigh against men with hairy chests who fill the beaches in summer. Like Addison De Witt, he is unsexed; having no gender of his own, he can switch from one sex to another as well as from one voice to another; even sounding like Mrs. Danvers in *Rebecca* (1940) as he issues orders to Milo, whom he reduces to a Mrs. de Winter—a rather ironic touch when one realizes that Olivier played Maxim de Winter in the movie version of *Rebecca*.

Milo, on the other hand, does not make a convincing woman. Rummaging around in the trunk, Andrew tosses him a gown, but Milo is clearly uncomfortable in drag. What captivates him, though, is the clown's costume; the childlike delight that Caine registers is affecting yet chilling. For within the social subtext of the film, Milo, by dressing as a clown, is conforming to Andrew's image of him. And within the sexual subtext, the prospect of Milo's having to change clothes in front of him makes Andrew giddily prurient: "Down to your smalls; don't be shy," he cackles, like a closet gay at a fraternity initiation.

To intensify the antagonism between the characters, Mankiewicz capitalized on the screen personae of Olivier and Caine: the lordly Shakespearean, now a lord himself; and the proud Cockney, born Maurice Joseph Micklewhite, the son of a Billingsgate fish porter and a cleaning woman. Two actors with less identifiable screen images would not have evoked the class tension that Shaffer wanted. Because of the casting, the film suggests the way a titled Englishman might treat the lower classes.

An actor who lacked Caine's jaunty confidence in his manhood would not succeed in making Milo's change from victim to tormenter plausible. The punishment that Milo inflicts on Andrew is more diabolical than the kind Andrew devised for him, for it was motivated by something Andrew could not understand; Andrew's game was a combined assault on Milo's manhood and his origins. The game made no distinction between Milo the male and Milo the man; it was based on the fact that Milo was a male, a sexually potent male, an Anglo-Italian, and therefore a threat to British superiority, sexual effeteness, and the Church of England. In the play, Milo planted three incriminating pieces of evidence in the living room, generously providing Andrew with riddling clues and giving him fifteen minutes to locate the objects: a crystal bracelet hidden in an ornamental tank; a shoe in a brightly decorated cornucopia; and a stocking in the clock.

In the film, Shaffer added a fourth object, made the hiding places more accessible, and gave Milo a cunning that was only implied in the play. The crystal bracelet is now in a wine glass; the stocking is wrapped around the shaft that drives the pendulum of the clock; the new object is a false eyelash in Jack Tar's eye; and the shoe is in the coal bin. One suspects the new location of the shoe was Mankiewicz's idea. The sight of Andrew clawing through coal recalls the humiliation that Biddle was to inflict on Luther in *No Way Out* until it was excised from the script. More than twenty years later, Mankiewicz had the opportunity to shoot his coal bin scene.

By making the riddles more complex (the clue to the stocking's location is contained in the lyrics to Cole Porter's "Anything Goes"), Shaffer is showing the ease with which a Milo Tindolini can become an Andrew Wyke—if not socially, then psychologically. Victim and victimizer, clown and ringmaster are twin faces of the same coin; spin it and they merge. For society, the implications of such a reversal are disturbing. An affront to an individual's or a group's ethnic origins, social class, or sexuality produces a mode of retaliation far deadlier than the vengeful fantasies of a writer because the impulse springs from a wounded psyche, not from the literary imagination. While Milo's revenge is framed within the life-as-theater setting, it is considerably more

real than Andrew's charade which, comparatively, is a more sophisticated version of the "Let's put on a show" syndrome of the Judy
Garland–Mickey Rooney MGM musicals.

When Andrew kills Milo the game is finished and the play is over.
Andrew's audience, the automata, rotate eerily, responding in the only
way they can before reverting to permanent stasis. But what they have
responded to is that heightened reality known as theater. The entire film
was a study in theater from the opening credits to the last shot of Andrew
in his living room that dissolves into a freeze, like the frieze-frames in
Cleopatra, turning into another sketch for the toy stage on which a
velvet curtain drops with the thud of a guillotine.

Sleuth is Mankiewicz's latest film to date. Whether there will be
another is problematical; his hopes of adapting Dee Wells's novel *Jane*
(1973) were dashed when the project collapsed. He often thinks of giving
up films entirely and devoting his time to writing a history of the stage
actress. Even if Mankiewicz makes another film, *Sleuth* will be his
summing up, just as *The Man Who Shot Liberty Valance* (1962) was John
Ford's although it was followed by three others.

Sleuth was the distillation of Mankiewicz's major themes: the battle of
wits between the aristocrat and the commoner; the interplay of reality
and illusion; the androgyny of the cunning; game as a species of theater;
and theater itself as a transcendent force capable of permeating every
level of life, existing in such diverse forms as a letter that keeps three
wives guessing and plot reversals that keep an audience guessing. *Sleuth*
pays homage to that force; it is theater on film.

However, this may not be much of a consolation to a man who still
wishes he had written for the stage and developed into another Philip
Barry. To be a playwright, one must master the art of dramatic (as
opposed to filmic) construction and stage dialogue. Yet one suspects that
All about Eve could never have succeeded on the stage, despite the
dialogue that made the critics swoon. *Eve's* structure was filmic; the
dialogue was the apotheosis of movie writing. *Eve* could have been a
play, but probably not a memorable one. In the dramatization that Orr
and Denham fashioned from the short story, "The Wisdom of Eve," one
can see what *Eve* might have been like on the stage. *The Wisdom of Eve,*
which has not been performed on Broadway although it was given an off
off-Broadway production in the summer of 1980, is one of those multiset
plays that tries to avoid multiple settings through a unit set that can
juxtapose Margo's dressing room and Karen's library, with the
downstage area serving as a television studio, a stage door, and a garden
entrance. It is also the kind of play that shows the stage monologue at its
most awkward, with Karen constantly speaking to and at the audience.

The best monologues turn exposition into revelation. For every monologue like Tom's in Williams's *The Glass Menagerie* that opens with "Yes, I have tricks in my pocket. I have things up my sleeve"; there is the "Ladies and Gentleman, I'm Mrs. Lloyd Roberts" type that opens *The Wisdom of Eve.*

Mankiewicz's monologues were thoroughly filmic, broken at the right point and given a rhythm suited to the medium, although probably not to literature. If he dramatized *Eve,* he undoubtedly would have written better dialogue than Orr and Denham. Yet one suspects he would have used the same structure as a carryover from screenwriting.

Fortunately, Mankiewicz never went into the theater. If he did, Broadway would have had a writer of drawing-room comedies who made an occasional detour into social drama and whose plays would have been so cinematic that the critics would have kept wondering why he had never written for the movies. Joseph L. Mankiewicz would not have been a loss to the stage; his loss to the movies would have constituted an artistic void. Mankiewicz's outstanding achievement was to perceive theater in filmic terms and to show that theater exists wherever life is raised above the mundane and people aspire to higher, although not necessarily to better, forms of themselves. For the elevation of the self means the elevation of everything connected with the self including language. Even the act of raising the vernacular to the level of stage dialogue is part of the transfiguring process known as theater.

If Mankiewicz still speculates on what lay at the end of the road not taken, he might find the answer in one of his favorite plays: "Fate, show thy force; ourselves we do not owe. / What is decreed must be— and be this so!" *(Twelfth Night,* act 1, scene 5).

Notes and References

Chapter One

1.   Richard Merryman, *Mank: The Wit, World, and Life of Herman Mankiewicz* (New York, 1978), p. 16.
2.   Kenneth L. Geist, *Pictures Will Talk: The Life and Films of Joseph L. Mankiewicz* (New York, 1978), p. 49.
3.   Gore Vidal, "Scott's Case," *New York Review of Books*, 1 May 1980, p. 18; see also Tom Dardis, *Some Time in the Sun: The Hollywood Years of Fitzgerald, Faulkner, Nathanael West, Aldous Huxley, and James Agee* (New York: Scribner's, 1976), pp. 37–44.
4.   Philip Dunne, *Take Two: A Life in Movies and Politics* (New York, 1980), p. 54.
5.   Nora Johnson, *Flashback: Nora Johnson on Nunnally Johnson* (New York: Doubleday, 1979), p. 121.

Chapter Three

1.   *Daily Variety*, 6 March 1962, p. 13.
2.   William K. Everson, *American Silent Film* (New York: Oxford University Press, 1978), pp. 23–24, describes a 1905 newsreel in which there is a 360-degree pan of a storm-wrecked waterfront in Galveston, Texas.
3.   Northrop Frye, *Anatomy of Criticism: Four Essays* (Princeton, N.J.: Princeton University Press, 1957), p. 169.

Chapter Five

1.   When *House of Strangers* was remade as a Western, *Broken Lance* (1954), Yordan won an Oscar for Best Motion Picture Story.

Chapter Six

1.   For a detailed account of the incident, see Geist, *Pictures Will Talk*, pp. 173–206; and Robert Parrish, *Growing Up in Hollywood* (New York, 1976), pp. 201–10.

2.   Gene D. Phillips, S.J., *Graham Greene: The Films of His Fiction* (New York: Columbia Teachers College Press, 1974), p. 135.
3.   Donald Lancaster, *The Emancipation of French Indochina* (New York: Oxford University Press, 1961), p. 234, n. 26.
4.   Letter to author, 9 June 1981.

Chapter Seven

1.   Although Vidal and Williams were given co-screenplay credit, the script was, for all practical purposes, Vidal's; Williams's name was "good for box office." See Bernard F. Dick, *The Apostate Angel: A Critical Study of Gore Vidal* (New York: Random House, 1974), p. 90.
2.   It is difficult to accept the view of Maurice Yacowar, *Tennessee Williams and Film* (New York: Ungar, 1977), p. 57, that Mankiewicz shaded the monologue surrealistically "to allow for the possibility that Catherine is relating a fantasy, not a memory." The monologue may seem surreal, but the visualization is not.

Chapter Eight

1.   On the revisions, see Geist, *Pictures Will Talk*, pp. 364–69.

Chapter Nine

1.   John Houseman, "This Our Lofty Scene," *Theatre Arts*, May, 1953, p. 28.
2.   In his otherwise exemplary *Shakespeare on Film* (Bloomington, 1977), Jack J. Jorgens takes an eccentric view of Louis Calhern's performance, claiming that the actor "portrays Caesar's weaknesses more than his strengths" (p. 96). Calhern portrayed neither.
3.   For the complete background, see Geist, *Pictures Will Talk*, pp. 302–45; Jack Brodsky and Nathan Weiss, *The Cleopatra Papers: A Private Correspondence* (New York: Simon and Schuster, 1963); Walter Wanger, *My Life with Cleopatra* (New York: Bantam Books, 1963).
4.   Robert Payne, "Then Antony Met Cleopatra," *New York Times Magazine*, 2 June 1963, p. 30.

Selected Bibliography

Primary Sources

1. Screenplay

Mankiewicz, Joseph L., and Carey, Gary. *More about All about Eve: A Colloquy by Gary Carey with Joseph L. Mankiewicz together with His Screenplay All about Eve*. New York: Random House, 1972. Indispensable. Carey's tracing of the film's genesis is almost as compelling as the script. For contrast, one might read Mary Orr and Reginald Denham's *The Wisdom of Eve* (New York: Dramatists Play Service, 1964), advertised as "adapted from the story by Mary Orr on which the film *All about Eve* was made."

2. Interviews

Bontemps, Jacques, and Overstreet, Richard. "Measure for Measure." *Cahiers du Cinéma in English* 8 (February 1967):28–41. The most satisfying interview Mankiewicz has given in which he maintains that "since cinema compromised itself by starting to talk, it has the obligation to say something."
Conrad, Derek. "Joseph Mankiewicz: Putting on the Style." *Films and Filming* 6 (January 1960):9, 33. Mankiewicz on his art: "I write essentially for audiences who come to listen to a film as well as to look at it."
Sarris, Andrew. "Mankiewicz of the Movies." *Show* 1 (March 1970):26–30, 78. Mankiewicz on the old moguls ("they were complete monsters") and the new breed ("the carpetbaggers").

Secondary Sources

1. Books

Dunne, Philip. *Take Two: A Life in Movies and Politics*. New York: McGraw-Hill, 1980. An absorbing autobiography as well as a cultural history of Hollywood by the screenwriter-director who wrote the scripts of three of Mankiewicz's films.
Geist, Kenneth L. *Pictures Will Talk: The Life and Films of Joseph L. Mankiewicz*. New York: Scribner's, 1978. As Louella Parsons used to say, it

"tells all." A biography—factual, anecdotal, and conjectural—interspersed with generally sound critical insights.

Gussow, Mel. *Don't Say Yes until I Finish Talking: A Biography of Darryl F. Zanuck.* New York: Doubleday, 1971. The man who hired, and once fired, Mankiewicz.

Jorgens, Jack J. *Shakespeare on Film.* Bloomington: Indiana University Press, 1977. An almost authoritative study, sensitive and scholarly, that perhaps asks more of *Julius Caesar* than Mankiewicz or anyone else could deliver.

Meryman, Richard. *Mank: The Wit, World, and Life of Herman Mankiewicz.* New York: Morrow, 1978. A model biography, human and moving, of the screenwriter that also describes Herman's relationship with his brother.

Parrish, Robert. *Growing Up in Hollywood.* New York: Harcourt Brace Jovanovich, 1976. Includes a vivid retelling of DeMille's attempt to oust Mankiewicz as SDG president in 1950.

2. Articles

Houseman, John. *"Julius Caesar*: Mr. Mankiewicz' Shooting Script." *Quarterly of Film, Radio and Television* 8 (Winter 1953):109–23. Contains the assassination sequence, its prelude and aftermath.

Pasinetti, P. M. *"Julius Caesar*: The Role of the Technical Adviser." *Quarterly of Film, Radio and Television* 8 (Winter 1953):131–39. Somewhat naive, yet one statement was prophetic: "Possibly the spectator . . . will be so taken by the exceptional quality of the directing and the acting that he will forget about . . . style, buildings, objects, props." All four were eminently forgettable.

Vidal, Gore. "Scott's Case." *New York Review of Books,* 1 May 1980, pp. 12–20. Documented account of Mankiewicz's role in the creation of the *Three Comrades* screenplay.

Filmography

DRAGONWYCK (Twentieth Century-Fox, 1946)
Producer: Ernst Lubitsch (uncredited)
Screenplay: Joseph L. Mankiewicz, from the novel by Anya Seton
Cinematographer: Arthur Miller
Art Direction: Lyle Wheeler, J. Russell Spencer
Music: Alfred Newman
Editor: Dorothy Spencer
Cast: Gene Tierney (Miranda Wells), Vincent Price (Nicholas Van Ryn), Walter Huston (Ephraim Wells), Anne Revere (Abigail Wells), Glenn Langan (Dr. Jeff Turner), Jessica Tandy (Peggy)
Running Time: 103 minutes
Released: April 1946
16mm. rental: Films Incorporated

SOMEWHERE IN THE NIGHT (Twentieth Century-Fox, 1946)
Producer: Anderson Lawler
Screenplay: Joseph L. Mankiewicz, Howard Dimsdale, from the story "The Lonely Journey" by Marvin Borowsky
Cinematographer: Norbert Brodine
Art Direction: James Basevi, Maurice Ransford
Music: David Buttolph, Emil Newman
Editor: James B. Clark
Cast: John Hodiak (George Taylor/Larry Cravat), Nancy Guild (Christy), Richard Conte (Mel Phillips), Lloyd Nolan (Lieutenant Kendall), Josephine Hutchinson (Elizabeth Conroy), Margo Woods (Phyllis)
Running Time: 100 minutes
Released: June 1946
16mm. rental: Films Incorporated

THE LATE GEORGE APLEY (Twentieth Century-Fox, 1947)
Producer: Fred Kohlmar
Screenplay: Philip Dunne, from the play by John P. Marquand and George S. Kaufman

Cinematographer: Joseph LaShelle
Art Direction: James Basevi, J. Russell Spencer
Music: Cyril Mockridge, Alfred Newman
Editor: James B. Clark
Cast: Ronald Colman (George Apley), Peggy Cummins (Eleanor Apley), Vanessa Brown (Agnes), Richard Haydn (Horatio), Edna Best (Catherine Apley), Percy Waram (Roger Newcombe), Mildred Natwick (Amelia), Richard Ney (John Apley), Charles Russell (Howard Boulder)
Running Time: 98 minutes
Released: March 1947
16mm. rental: Films Incorporated

THE GHOST AND MRS. MUIR (Twentieth Century-Fox, 1947)
Producer: Fred Kohlmar
Screenplay: Philip Dunne, from the novel by R. A. Dick (Josephine Aimee Campbell Leslie)
Cinematographer: Charles Lang
Art Direction: Richard Day, George Davis
Music: Bernard Herrmann
Editor: Dorothy Spencer
Cast: Gene Tierney (Lucy Muir), Rex Harrison (Captain Daniel Gregg), George Sanders (Miles Fairley), Edna Best (Martha), Vanessa Brown (Anna Muir), Natalie Wood (Anna Muir, as a child), Anna Lee (Mrs. Miles Fairley)
Running Time: 104 minutes
Released: June 1947
16mm. rental: Films Incorporated

ESCAPE (Twentieth Century-Fox, 1948)
Producer: William Perlberg
Screenplay: Philip Dunne, from the play by John Galsworthy
Cinematographer: Frederick A. Young
Art Direction: Vetchinsky
Music: William Alwyn. Music played by the Philharmonia Orchestra of London
Editor: Alan L. Jaggs
Cast: Rex Harrison (Matt Denant), Peggy Cummins (Dora Winton), Jill Esmond (Grace Winton), William Hartnell (Inspector Harris), Norman Wooland (Parson)
Running Time: 78 minutes
Released: June 1948
16mm. rental: Films Incorporated

A LETTER TO THREE WIVES (Twentieth Century-Fox, 1949)
Producer: Sol C. Siegel
Screenplay: Joseph L. Mankiewicz, from a *Cosmopolitan* magazine story by John Klempner
Adaptation: Vera Caspary
Cinematographer: Arthur Miller
Art Direction: Lyle Wheeler, J. Russell Spencer

Music: Alfred Newman
Editor: J. Watson Webb, Jr.
Cast: Jeanne Crain (Deborah Bishop), Linda Darnell (Lora May Hollingsway),
Ann Sothern (Rita Phipps), Kirk Douglas (George Phipps), Paul Douglas (Porter
Hollingsway), Barbara Lawrence (Babe), Jeffrey Lynn (Brad Bishop), Connie
Gilchrist (Mrs. Finney), Thelma Ritter (Sadie), Florence Bates (Mrs. Manleigh),
Hobart Cavanaugh (Mr. Manleigh), Celeste Holm (Voice of Addie Ross)
Running Time: 103 minutes
Released: January 1949
16mm. rental: Films Incorporated

HOUSE OF STRANGERS (Twentieth Century-Fox, 1949)
Producer: Sol C. Siegel
Screenplay: Joseph L. Mankiewicz (uncredited), Philip Yordan, from a chapter
of the novel *I'll Never Go There Any More* by Jerome Weidman
Cinematographer: Milton Krasner
Art Direction: Lyle Wheeler, George W. Davis
Music: Daniele Amfitheatrof
Editor: Harmon Jones
Cast: Edward G. Robinson (Gino Monetti), Richard Conte (Max Monetti), Susan
Hayward (Irene Bennett), Luther Adler (Joe Monetti), Efrem Zimbalist, Jr.
(Tony Monetti), Paul Valentine (Pietro Monetti), Esther Minciotti (Theresa
Monetti), Hope Emerson (Helena)
Running Time: 101 minutes
Released: July 1949
16mm. rental: Films Incorporated

NO WAY OUT (Twentieth Century-Fox, 1950)
Producer: Darryl F. Zanuck
Screenplay: Joseph L. Mankiewicz, Lesser Samuels
Cinematographer: Milton Krasner
Art Direction: Lyle Wheeler, George W. Davis
Music: Alfred Newman
Editor: Barbara McLean
Cast: Richard Widmark (Ray Biddle), Linda Darnell (Edie), Stephen McNally
(Dr. Wharton), Sidney Poitier (Dr. Luther Brooks), Mildred Joanne Smith
(Cora Brooks), Harry Bellaver (George Biddle), Ruby Dee (Connie), Ossie
Davis (John)
Running Time: 106 minutes
Released: August 1950
16mm. rental: Films Incorporated

ALL ABOUT EVE (Twentieth Century-Fox, 1950)
Producer: Darryl F. Zanuck
Screenplay: Joseph L. Mankiewicz, from a *Cosmopolitan* magazine story by
Mary Orr
Cinematographer: Milton Krasner
Art Direction: Lyle Wheeler, George W. Davis

Music: Alfred Newman
Editor: Barbara McLean
Cast: Bette Davis (Margo Channing), Anne Baxter (Eve Harrington), George Sanders (Addison De Witt), Celeste Holm (Karen Richards), Gary Merrill (Bill Sampson), Hugh Marlowe (Lloyd Richards), Thelma Ritter (Birdie), Marilyn Monroe (Miss Caswell), Gregory Ratoff (Max Fabian), Barbara Bates (Phoebe), Walter Hampden (Aged Actor)
Running Time: 138 minutes
Released: October 1950
16mm. rental: Films Incorporated

PEOPLE WILL TALK (Twentieth Century-Fox, 1951)
Producer: Darryl F. Zanuck
Screenplay: Joseph L. Mankiewicz, from the play by Curt Goetz
Cinematographer: Milton Krasner
Art Direction: Lyle Wheeler, George W. Davis
Music: Alfred Newman
Editor: Barbara McLean
Cast: Cary Grant (Dr. Noah Praetorius), Jeanne Crain (Deborah Higgins), Finlay Currie (Shunderson), Hume Cronyn (Dr. Rodney Elwell), Walter Slezak (Professor Lionel Parker), Sidney Blackmer (Arthur Higgins), Will Wright (John Higgins), Margaret Hamilton (Sarah Pickett)
Running Time: 110 minutes
Released: August 1951
16mm. rental: Films Incorporated

FIVE FINGERS (Twentieth Century-Fox, 1952)
Producer: Otto Lang
Screenplay: Michael Wilson, from the book *Operation Cicero* by L. C. Moyzisch
Cinematographer: Norbert Brodine
Art Direction: Lyle Wheeler, George W. Davis
Music: Bernard Herrmann
Editor: James B. Clark
Cast: James Mason (Diello), Danielle Darrieux (Countess Anna Staviska), Michael Rennie (Colin Travers), Walter Hampden (Sir Frederic), Oscar Karlweis (Moyzisch), Herbert Berghof (von Richter), John Wengraf (von Papen)
Running Time: 108 minutes
Released: February 1952
16mm. rental: Films Incorporated

JULIUS CAESAR (Metro-Goldwyn-Mayer, 1953)
Producer: John Houseman
Cinematographer: Joseph Ruttenberg
Art Direction: Cedric Gibbons, Edward Carfagno, Edwin B. Willis, Hugh Hunt
Music: Miklós Rósza
Editor: John Dunning
Cast: Marlon Brando (Mark Antony), James Mason (Brutus), John Gielgud (Cassius), Louis Calhern (Caesar), Edmond O'Brien (Casca), Deborah Kerr

(Portia), Greer Garson (Calpurnia), Douglas Watson (Octavius), Edmond Pur-
dom (Strato)
Running Time: 120 minutes
Released: June 1953
16mm. rental: Films Incorporated

THE BAREFOOT CONTESSA (United Artists, 1954)
Producer: Joseph L. Mankiewicz
Screenplay: Joseph L. Mankiewicz
Cinematographer: Jack Cardiff
Art Direction: Arrigo Equini
Music: Mario Nascimbene
Editor: William Hornbeck
Cast: Humphrey Bogart (Harry Dawes), Ava Gardner (Maria Vargas), Edmond
O'Brien (Oscar Muldoon), Marius Goring (Alberto Bravano), Valentina Cortesa
(Eleonora Torlato-Favrini), Rossano Brazzi (Vincenzo Torlato-Favrini), Warren
Stevens (Kirk Edwards), Mari Aldon (Myrna)
Running Time: 128 minutes
Released: September 1954
16mm. rental: MGM/UA

GUYS AND DOLLS (Goldwyn/MGM, 1955)
Producer: Samuel Goldwyn
Screenplay: Joseph L. Mankiewicz, from the musical with book by Jo Swerling
and Abe Burrows
Music and Lyrics: Frank Loesser
Choreography: Michael Kidd
Cinematographer: Harry Stradling
Art Direction: Oliver Smith, Joseph Wright, Howard Bristol
Editor: Daniel Mandel
Cast: Marlon Brando (Sky Masterson), Jean Simmons (Sarah Brown), Frank
Sinatra (Nathan Detroit), Vivian Blaine (Miss Adelaide), Robert Keith (Lieuten-
ant Brannigan), Stubby Kaye (Nicely-Nicely Johnson), B. S. Pully (Big Julie),
Regis Toomey (Arvid Abernathy)
Running Time: 150 minutes
Released: November 1955
16mm. rental: Twyman

THE QUIET AMERICAN (United Artists, 1958)
Producer: Joseph L. Mankiewicz
Screenplay: Joseph L. Mankiewicz, from the novel by Graham Greene
Cinematographer: Robert Krasker
Art Direction: Rino Mondellini, Dario Simoni
Music: Mario Nascimbene
Editor: William Hornbeck
Cast: Audie Murphy (The American), Michael Redgrave (Thomas Fowler),
Claude Dauphin (Vigot), Giorgia Moll (Phuong), Bruce Cabot (Bill Granger),
Richard Loo (Mr. Heng)

Running Time: 120 minutes
Released: February 1958
16mm. rental: MGM/UA

SUDDENLY, LAST SUMMER (Columbia, 1959)
Producer: Sam Spiegel
Screenplay: Gore Vidal, Tennessee Williams, from the play by Tennessee Williams
Cinematographer: Jack Hildyard
Art Direction: Oliver Messel
Music: Buxton Orr, Malcolm Arnold
Editor: William Hornbeck
Cast: Elizabeth Taylor (Catherine Holly), Montgomery Clift (Dr. Cukrowicz), Katharine Hepburn (Violet Venable), Mercedes McCambridge (Mrs. Holly), Albert Dekker (Dr. Hockstader)
Running Time: 114 minutes
Released: December 1959
16mm. rental: Twyman

CLEOPATRA (Twentieth Century-Fox, 1963)
Producer: Walter Wanger
Screenplay: Joseph L. Mankiewicz, Ranald MacDougall, Sidney Buchman, based upon the histories of Plutarch, Suetonius, Appian, and other ancient sources and *The Life and Times of Cleopatra* by C. M. Franzero
Cinematographer: Leon Shamroy
Art Direction: Jack Martin Smith, Hilyard Brown, Herman Blumenthal, Elven Webb, Maurice Pelling, Boris Juraga
Music: Alex North
Choreography: Hermes Pan
Editor: Dorothy Spencer
Cast: Elizabeth Taylor (Cleopatra), Richard Burton (Mark Antony), Rex Harrison (Julius Caesar), Pamela Brown (High Priestess), Sosigenes (Hume Cronyn), Apollodorus (Cesare Danova), Kenneth Haigh (Brutus), Martin Landau (Rufio), Roddy McDowall (Octavian), Robert Stephens (Germanicus), Isabelle Cooley (Charmian), Michael Hordern (Cicero), Jean Marsh (Octavia)
Running Time: 243 minutes
Released: June 1963
16mm. rental: Films Incorporated

THE HONEY POT (United Artists, 1967)
Producers: Charles K. Feldman, Joseph L. Mankiewicz
Screenplay: Joseph L. Mankiewicz, from the play *Mr. Fox of Venice* by Frederick Knott, based on Thomas Sterling's novel *The Evil of the Day,* inspired by Ben Jonson's *Volpone*
Cinematographer: Gianni Di Venanzo
Art Direction: John DeCuir
Music: John Addison
Editor: David Bretherton

Cast: Rex Harrison (Cecil Fox), Susan Hayward (Lone Star), Cliff Robertson (McFly), Capucine (Dominique), Edie Adams (Merle McGill), Maggie Smith (Sarah Watkins), Adolfo Celi (Inspector Rizzi)
Running Time: 131 minutes
Released: May 1967
16mm. rental: MGM/UA

THERE WAS A CROOKED MAN (Warner Brothers, 1970)
Producer: Joseph L. Mankiewicz
Screenplay: David Newman, Robert Benton
Cinematographer: Harry Stradling, Jr.
Art Direction: Edward Carrere
Music: Charles Strouse
Title Song: Charles Strouse, Lee Adams
Editor: Gene Milford
Cast: Kirk Douglas (Paris Pitman, Jr.), Henry Fonda (Woodward Lopeman), Hume Cronyn (Dudley Whinner), Warren Oates (Floyd Moon), Burgess Meredith (Missouri Kid), Lee Grant (Mrs. Bullard), Arthur O'Connell (Mr. Lomax), Martin Gabel (Warden Le Goff), John Randolph (Cyrus McNutt)
Running Time: 125 minutes
Released: December 1970
16mm. rental: Audio Brandon/Films Incorporated

SLEUTH (Twentieth Century-Fox, 1972)
Producer: Morton Gottlieb
Screenplay: Anthony Shaffer, based on his play
Cinematographer: Oswald Morris
Art Direction: Peter Lamont
Music: John Addison
Editor: Richard Marden
Cast: Laurence Olivier (Andrew Wyke), Michael Caine (Milo Tindle) [Alec Cawthorne (Inspector Doppler), Eve Channing (Marguerite), John Matthews (Detective Sergeant Tarrant), Karen Minfort-Jones (Teya), Teddy Martin (Police Constable Higgs)]
Running Time: 138 minutes
Released: December 1972
16mm. rental: Films Incorporated

Television Play

CAROL FOR ANOTHER CHRISTMAS (Xerox Corporation/Telsun Foundation, Inc., for the United Nations, 1964)
Producer and Director: Joseph L. Mankiewicz
Screenplay: Rod Serling, from the novel *A Christmas Carol* by Charles Dickens
Photography: Arthur Ornitz
Art Director: Gene Callahan
Music: Henry Mancini

Editor: Robert Lawrence
Cast: Sterling Hayden (Daniel Grudge), Peter Fonda (Morley), Ben Gazzara (Fred), Richard Harris (Ghost of Christmas Present), Steve Lawrence (Ghost of Christmas Past), Eva Marie Saint (Wave), Peter Sellers (Imperial Me), Joseph Wiseman (Ghost of Christmas Future)
Aired: 28 December 1964 (ABC-TV)
Can only be viewed at the Visual Materials Library of the United Nations.

Index